WHY WE LOVE COFFEE

FUN FACTS, HISTORY, AND CULTURE OF THE WORLD'S MOST POPULAR DRINK

mango
PUBLISHING GROUP

COFFEE MUST BE HOT AS HELL,
BLACK AS THE DEVIL,
PURE AS AN ANGEL AND SWEET AS LOVE.

- Mikhail Alexandrovich Bakunin -

TEXT BY LUIGI ODELLO

PHOTOGRAPHS BY FABIO PETRONI

RECIPES BY CHEF GIOVANNI RUGGIERI

Project editor VALERIA MANFERTO DE FABIANIS

Editorial assistant LAURA ACCOMAZZO

Graphic design MARIA CUCCHI

CONTENTS

6-7 Detail of a 1855 Viennese coffee machine.
14-15 An old coffee grinder.

WHY WE LOVE COFFEE

PAIRING COFFEE AND FOOD
20 RECIPES BY CHEF GIOVANNI RUGGIERI

COFFEE

Simply extraordinary. What, you ask? The answer is coffee, of course. And the reasons why it's so extraordinary are not hard to explain.

Among the world's most popular beverages, coffee made its debut around the 14th century in Yemen, where it was cultivated. But roughly a century earlier, in Ethiopia – coffee's birthplace – the plant grew wild. Why it took coffee so long to become a consumer commodity remains a mystery, but what's clear is that today, coffee stands as the world's second-most traded commodity, right after oil. We consume about 700 billion cups of coffee annually, made from over 137 million hundredweights (7 billion kilograms) of green coffee harvested from more than 30 million farms in 75 countries across the tropical coffee belt. These numbers are staggering, especially considering they represent less than two centuries of coffee's journey: in 1825, coffee production was about ninety times smaller, and today it continues its upward trajectory.

This global phenomenon originates from the Coffea, a shrub that botanists categorize under the Rubiaceae family. It diversifies into over ninety species, but only two dominate global production: Coffea Arabica and Coffea Canephora (commonly referred to as Robusta coffee). Due to natural mutations and human expertise, these species have given rise to over seventy coffee varieties. Factor in variations due to regional conditions like climate, sunlight, and soil, and the number of coffee types nearly matches that of grape wines. But there's more: consider the diverse farming methods, harvesting practices, and coffee bean processing. From naturally growing coffee plants in forest shade to expansive organized plantations, from selectively hand-picked cherries to machine harvesting, each method produces a unique taste in our coffee cup.

Another remarkable feature of coffee is that typically, only the seeds (what we know as coffee beans) of the coffee cherry are utilized, discarding the pulp. This fruit – scientifically termed the drupe – comprises an external skin, a sweet pulp, and usually two seeds (though sometimes just one) with their flat sides touching. To create the coffee we're familiar with, the beans are separated from the pulp. This can be done using three distinct methods, resulting in unwashed, semi-washed, or washed coffee.

After stripping the beans of their parchment and silver skin, they're ready for roasting. This stage introduces other vital factors influencing the taste and aroma of our coffee: varying techniques, durations, and temperatures produce distinct sensory experiences and flavors. Following roasting, the beans are ground – a pivotal step, though not as critical as brewing. At least ten unique methods exist for preparing a coffee cup, each with its signature attributes.

In essence: no matter the effort, a single lifetime isn't sufficient to savor all the coffee varieties available. And we haven't even delved into the myriad combinations coffee can be a part of, whether with milk, liquors, or other mix-ins.

That's why coffee is, indeed, so extraordinary.

WHERE IS COFFEE CULTIVATED AND HOW

THE PLANT, THE PLANTS

The genus *Coffea* encompasses an incredible variety of species, but only two stand out for producing fruits suitable for human consumption: Arabica and Canephora, the latter better known as Robusta. These two species flourish in distinct climates, and most importantly, they produce very different brews.

ROBUSTA

Robusta, or Canephora, might be less popular than Arabica and considered less refined, but it's notably resilient, especially against pests. Its name "Robusta" stems from its robust nature, a trait reflected in its more bitter, astringent, and full-bodied brew compared to Arabica. It's thanks to its higher caffeine (2–3.5%) and phenolic acid content. Wild Robusta plants can tower between 23 to 42 feet, although cultivated plants are shorter. These plants have slender elliptical leaves and grow notably round cherries. They thrive between 650 and 1900 feet in altitude, preferring consistent temperatures of 75°F to 85°F. As one of the earliest species on Earth, Robusta has 24 chromosomes and requires external pollination.

ARABICA

Arabica is more widespread, though Robusta is gaining ground, largely due to its resilience against chang-
ing climates and growing demand for lower-quality coffee. Wild Arabica plants range from 9 to 16 feet
in height but are often limited to 6 to 9 feet on farms for easier harvesting. Arabica cherries house two
beans, and the plant thrives between 2900 and 6500 feet where temperatures linger between 60°F and
75°F. Beans from Arabica contain less caffeine (0.7–2%) but have more sugars and fats, making them a
top choice for coffee lovers. Interestingly, Arabica plants became self-pollinating when their chromosome
count doubled, though cross-pollination does occur occasionally.

Much like wine grapes, coffee has numerous varieties. Over time, Arabica and Robusta have evolved
into different sub-species, many resulting from cross-breeding. It's often more challenging to categorize
coffee than wine, as coffee varieties sometimes derive their names from regions, leading to confusion
about whether the name represents a location or a genetic variation.

The Coffee Tree.

Below are descriptions of notable varieties among the many Arabica and Canephora variants:

BOURBON: This cultivar led to many Arabica varieties. Originating in the 18th century on Réunion Island (formerly Île Bourbon), it later spread to Brazil and then across the Americas. Red, Yellow, and Pink Bourbons are its sub-species.

CATIMOR: Developed in 1959 in Portugal to combat plant pathogens, Catimor is a cross between Caturra (an Arabica variant) and Timor, a natural Arabica-Robusta hybrid. Its beans sometimes have an unappealing herbaceous note.

CATUAI: Introduced in Brazil in the 1950s, this variety is a cross between Caturra and Mundo Novo, yielding a good bean quality.

CATURRA: Originating from a Bourbon mutation found in Brazil in the 19th century, Caturra is more productive due to its shorter stature and denser branches.

COLOMBIA: This variety was developed to resist certain diseases.

GEISHA or Gesha: Although named after an Ethiopian village, the most prized (and pricey) Geisha coffee, renowned for its sensory qualities, hails from Panama.

MARAGOGYPE: A Typica mutation characterized by its lush foliage and large seeds.

MUNDO NOVO: A prevalent variety in Brazil, resulting from a Bourbon and Typica cross, known for its high yield.

PACAMARA: This Salvadoran hybrid from 1958 combines the Pacas and Maragogype species.

PACAS: A natural Bourbon mutation.

SL28 AND SL34: Developed in Kenya's Scott Laboratories during the 1930s, these plants produce beans with distinct citrusy notes.

TIMOR: A natural Arabica and Robusta hybrid discovered on the island of Timor in the 1940s.

TYPICA: One of the original coffee varietals, which adapted to various climates, leading to the Kona (Hawaii) and Blue Mountain (Jamaica) varieties.

COFFEE – ITS TRAVELS THROUGH THE CENTURIES

Most historians generally agree that the ancient province of Kaffa in southwestern Ethiopia was the birthplace of coffee, likely originating during the early centuries of the last millennium. The first coffee plantation was established in Harar, situated at an elevation of 6000 feet (1885 meters) above sea level.

The reason behind coffee's gradual journey from obscurity to becoming a household staple remains a mystery. However, what is known is that its widespread popularity and success were driven by the physiological effects induced by the beverage brewed from its beans and seeds. Legend has it that these effects were initially observed by a shepherd who noticed his goats becoming rather lively after consuming some coffee leaves from the plant (as they too contain caffeine). Alternatively, it is more plausible that human curiosity led someone in pursuit of new flavors to sample the coffee cherries. Regardless of the circumstances, coffee was celebrated as one of nature's remarkable gifts.

One of the many coffee posters Belgian artist Marc-Henri Meunier designed
for Rajan in 1899.

WHERE IS COFFEE CULTIVATED AND HOW

*Coffea Arabica leaves
and flowers.*

In the fourteenth century, Yemen boasted coffee cultivations, and the fruits were used to create a beverage that enhanced alertness and resistance to fatigue.

Over the next two centuries, coffee's reach extended throughout the Middle East. Its spread mirrored the growth of Islam – a religion that, having forbidden alcoholic beverages, embraced this invigorating drink. The drink also took on ritual significance, setting this culture apart from Christianity. Coffee then made its way to India, in the Mysore region, introduced by Baba Budan, a pilgrim who had smuggled seven raw coffee beans out of Mecca.

In the seventeenth century, some Dutch traders acquired coffee seedlings. These were initially planted in Amsterdam's botanical gardens before being transferred to the East Indies, leading to the establishment of the famed Java and Sumatra plantations. In the early eighteenth century, French officer Gabriel de Clieu undertook the mission of transporting a coffee seedling – a gift from Amsterdam's Burgomaster to King Louis XIV – to Martinique. This venture was a success, marking the beginning of coffee plantations in the New World. Remarkably, within just fifty years, the island was home to nearly twenty million coffee plants. Around the same time, recognizing the potential of coffee plantations, the British commenced their own cultivations in Jamaica and India. However, the British weren't the only Europeans investing in coffee. The French also tried their hand at coffee cultivation in Guyana, although their venture met with less success. As legend has it, a man named Francisco de Melo Palheta seduced the wife of the governor in 1727, who then gifted him some coffee seedlings. These seedlings, transported to Brazil, marked the start of what would become the world's largest coffee production.

By 1740, coffee had made its way to Mexico and reached Venezuela by 1784. Around the same time, it was introduced to Colombia. The nineteenth century saw a significant rise in African coffee cultivations, spreading to nations like Congo and Madagascar, as well as Rwanda, Burundi, and Tanganyika (a German East-Africa colony back then), among others.

WHERE IS COFFEE CULTIVATED?

Coffee is cultivated in over seventy-five countries worldwide. With few exceptions, all these countries are situated between the Tropic of Cancer and the Tropic of Capricorn. The origin of coffee beans is significant as it distinguishes them in the market. Indeed, consumers often base their choice on origin, particularly those who've globetrotted to sample various qualities, only to return to savor the unmatched Italian Espresso blend – especially when certified. In some instances, a coffee's origin aligns with distinct characteristics because certain regions correspond to specific climatic conditions, coffee species and varieties, and raw bean processing methods. However, sometimes origin is merely a means to explore new coffee varieties.

Poll a hundred travelers returning from Brazil about the renowned Brazilian Santos, and you'll likely receive a hundred varied responses. That's because Santos refers to the port where the coffee is amassed. The coffee originates from across a nation as vast as a continent, spanning 2,730 miles from north to south and 2,684 miles from east to west, thereby encompassing a remarkable variety of coffees.

While Brazil, as the world's leading coffee producer, stands out, the same concept applies to all equatorial coffee-producing nations. Coffee classified by origin – be it Ethiopia, Colombia, India, or another – naturally covers an array of distinct productions. This perspective shifts slightly when referencing a smaller region or even a specific plantation (a finca) from a particular year. Here, the interplay of a singular species, varietal, soil, and climate, combined with consistent cultural factors, tends to guarantee a distinct sensory profile – as long as the roasting method remains constant and doesn't introduce variability.

Coffee plants thrive in mild heat and high humidity, so their growth is restricted to the "coffee bean belt" between 22° North and 22° South. Within this zone, different species, along with varied soil conditions and cultivation methods, contribute to significant disparities in coffee production across countries. Arabica favors seasonal shifts and prospers in regions where temperatures oscillate between 59°F and 74°F (15–23°C). In contrast, Robusta can't withstand these temperature fluctuations and favors consistent temperatures of 75°F to 85°F (24–29°C), typical of the equatorial zone (between 10° North and 10° South). Environmental factors profoundly affect coffee's sensory attributes. A primary distinction is between high-altitude and low-altitude coffee. Arabica plantations are best situated between 2,900 and 6,500 feet (900–2,000 meters) above sea level, while Robusta prefers elevations of 650 to 1,900 feet (200–600 meters).

Conventionally, in areas near the equator, the benchmark for higher-quality coffee is set around 4,900 feet (1,500 meters). Beyond this altitude, the beans generally have a greater specific weight, often referred to as "hard beans." This leads to classifications such as SHB (Strictly Hard Beans) and SHG (Strictly High Grown). As the altitude decreases, so does the density of the beans, resulting in what are known as "soft beans." The increased specific weight at these higher altitudes can be attributed to unique climatic conditions, varying sun exposure, and temperature fluctuations. These factors lead to a higher concentration of fats, sugars, and proteins in the seed, which eventually becomes the coffee bean. However, when plantations are situated closer to the tropics, these premium conditions can be present at significantly lower altitudes, sometimes even below 2,900 feet (900 meters) above sea level.

Environmental conditions that facilitate the slow ripening of fruit often lead to seeds with a higher concentration of sugars, organic acids, amino acids, and fats. These components then produce aroma precursors that can be amplified in subsequent stages of raw bean processing and roasting. For instance, terpenes and diterpenes can give rise to floral aromas. Social stability also plays a pivotal role in the quality of coffee produced. Coffee plants take years to mature, and their plantations demand ongoing care. If a region faces social turmoil, it becomes challenging to adequately manage coffee plantations and processing plants, which in turn adversely affects the final product. Throughout recent coffee history, numerous examples exist of coffee varieties that were once prevalent but have become increasingly scarce, such as the Yemen or Congo varietals.

In the future, we might find ourselves sipping on coffees strikingly different from the ones we're familiar with today, oblivious to the reasons behind this transformation. The situation, while complex, has a few dis-

A unique climate allows the cultivation of coffee on the hills of Manizales in Colombia.

cernible focal points. As climate change causes temperatures to rise, Arabica coffee may be forced to migrate to cooler, higher grounds or further from the equator. This would potentially shield the crops from pathogens that proliferate in warmer climates, which the plants are ill-equipped to combat. However, either way, Arabica stands at a disadvantage. The feasible solution might lie in developing resistant hybrids, which could unfortunately strip Arabica of the very attributes that make it so cherished among aficionados. Already, 80% of coffee cultivated in Colombia belongs to the Catimor variety – resilient, yet notably marked by persistent woody undertones. In Brazil, emergent Robusta varieties could even flourish in the Amazon, offering vast new expanses for coffee farming with staggering average yields surpassing 15,000 lbs (7,000 kilograms) per hectare. The downside? A product lacking in robust sensory properties.

Another pivotal consideration is the rise of new coffee-producing nations like China, which is already introducing over 132 million lbs (60 million kilograms) of coffee to the market. Meanwhile, nations historically celebrated for their premium coffee, such as India and Mexico, are seeing diminished exports due to surging domestic consumption. It seems that as living standards ascend, so does the preference for coffee over alternative beverages, further dwindling the availability of premium coffee in the market. A glimmer of hope, however, might lie in the evolution of African coffee production, particularly Canephora, given the implementation of modern processing techniques.

Indeed, one element poised to significantly alter coffee's sensory profile – especially in the exacting realm of espresso – is the methodologies employed for drupe selection and raw bean processing. Hand-picked harvests, ensuring cherries are plucked at their ripest, are nearing obsolescence. Consequently, a staggering 80% of harvested fruits lack optimal sugar levels, whereas premium coffee necessitates overripe cherries brimming with simple sugars. Hence, akin to grape selection in winemaking, there's an imperative to meticulously grade coffee cherries based on quality.

Meanwhile, as technology continues to influence agricultural practices, we're witnessing a decline in the prevalence of washed coffee and its hallmark fresh, fruity/floral nuances. Furthermore, the drying durations for natural coffees are diminishing – a detrimental trend for quality. This is because it curtails the endogenous fermentation of cherries and prematurely halts the enzymatic activity vital for generating aroma precursors. It's no surprise, then, that Brazil is pioneering the use of intermittent dryers, designed to nurture embryonic development prior to germ deactivation.

Given these insights, let's now turn our attention to the most significant coffee origins, be it by volume or rarity, or the ones we're most likely to spot on packaging labels.

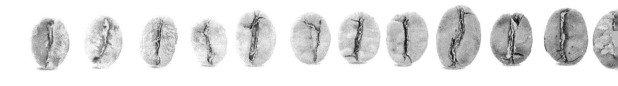

BRAZILIAN MOGIANA

A prominent name amongst Brazil's stellar coffee-producing regions, Mogiana often falls under the broader category of Santos - named after the traditional export port for Brazilian coffee. Nestled in the State of São Paulo and sharing its borders with Minas Gerais, Mogiana is intricately subdivided into Alta (High), Média (Mid), and Baixa (Low) regions. Historically, the Alta and Média regions have been celebrated for their high-quality coffee: a pristine natural Arabica renowned for its robust body, harmonious acidity, and a unique aromatic blend of cocoa and chocolate.

The Mogiana Paulista boasts a temperate climate, averaging around 68 °F (20 °C). Annual rainfall measures approximately 5.5 feet (1700 millimeters), predominantly during spring and autumn. This leaves a dry spell from May to September, conveniently coinciding with the coffee harvest and subsequent drupe drying period.

Rich in iron, the region's sandy terrains exhibit a distinct red hue and span altitudes ranging from 2400 to 3900 feet (750–1200 meters). While Catuai and Mundo Novo are the predominant varieties, harvesting these cherries – increasingly done using sophisticated machinery – is facilitated by the region's mild inclines and systematic plantation layouts. Regardless of the harvesting technique – manual or mechanized – the cherries undergo drying on the ground using the "dry" method. They're meticulously spread out and flipped as many as thirteen times daily to deter undesirable fermentations. Although ovens are sometimes employed, they often hinder optimal enzyme formation.

CAMEROON ROBUSTA GG SUPERIOR

Venturing to the West African nation of Cameroon, especially the province of Ebolowa, one encounters a relatively cooler climate. A single rainy season extends from July to November. Approximately 2200 feet (700 meters) above sea level, the soil – bearing striking similarities to volcanic terrain – nurtures Robusta varietals, originally from Zaire. These cherries are diligently hand-picked between November and February, then naturally processed to extract the beans. Once roasted, the beans perfectly encapsulate the Robusta essence: a robust body, subdued acidity, and a pronounced bitterness. Flavor profiles evoke toasted bread, cocoa, chocolate, and a characteristic ashy undertone. Yet, among Robustas, its taste stands out as exceptionally crisp.

COLOMBIA MEDELLIN SUPREMO

In the nineteenth century, Colombia's coffee industry underwent a significant transformation when it was introduced to coffee plants from the French Antilles,

inadvertently leading to a mixture of coffee varieties. Over the past century, Colombia has risen to become the world's second-largest coffee producer and the foremost producer of washed Arabica beans.

Nestled in the Medellin region, at the foothills of the Andes and an elevation of approximately 5,200 feet (1,600 meters) above sea level, you'll find thriving coffee plantations that cultivate some of the finest Colombian coffees. The climate in this region is subtropical, characterized by humidity, moderate ventilation, and an average annual rainfall of 5.4 feet (1,650 mm). Average annual temperatures hover around 72 °F (22 °C), with variations ranging from 61 °F to 99 °F (16–37 °C). The predominantly volcanic soil in this area is home to various coffee varieties, both old and more recent.

Colombia Medellin Supremo undergoes two annual harvests, one between April and May, followed by the primary one between October and December. Skilled workers manually pick the ripe drupes during these periods. The yield is relatively modest, producing just over 15,000 lbs (7,000 kilograms) per hectare. The processing of green coffee beans follows the "wet" method, which involves fermenting the pulp from the drupes and subsequently drying the seeds.

Despite being a washed coffee, Colombia Medellin Supremo boasts a robust body and limited acidity. Its aroma is characterized by notes of fresh fruit, chocolate, toasted bread, biscuits, and walnut, with the latter note occasionally taking center stage.

COSTARICA SHB TARRAZU

Coffee was introduced to Costa Rica from Cuba and the Antilles during the eighteenth century. The region of Tarrazu, comprising its three subzones: San Marcos, San Lorenzo, and San Carlos, emerged as a particularly favorable environment for coffee cultivation, yielding beans of the highest quality.

The climate in Tarrazu alternates between two distinct seasons: a wet season from May to November, characterized by an average rainfall of 7.8 feet (2,400 mm), and a dry season from December to April. Temperatures oscillate between 63°F and 83°F (17°C-28°C), with an average hovering around 66°F (19°C). Enriched by volcanic origins, the humus-rich and mineral-laden soil sits at altitudes ranging from 3,900 feet (1,200 meters) to 6,200 feet (1,900 meters) above sea level. The latter altitude reaches the threshold to qualify as a Strictly Hard Bean. Predominantly, Caturra and Catuai varieties are grown – strictly Arabica, as Costa Rica has outlawed Robusta cultivation. These coffee plants thrive under the canopy of towering trees, and their drupes, harvested in the dry season, undergo wet-method pulping before being sun-dried in open courtyards or on mats. The resulting beans are high-density, lustrous, flat, and display a greenish-blue hue.

When roasted adeptly, this coffee variety unfolds into an intriguing and sophisticated brew. It presents a dry and slightly bitter profile, balanced with vibrant acidity. Its aromatic composition evokes distinct notes of fresh, desiccated, and dried fruits, occasionally accompanied by undertones of balsamic and spice.

ETHIOPIA YIRGACHEFFE

This is a prestigious coffee originally from the Gedeo zone surrounding the city of Yirgacheffe, situated at 6,200 feet (1,900 meters) above sea level. The Arabica plantations lie between 5,500 and 8,200 feet (1,700–2,500 meters) on volcanic soil that is incredibly rich in minerals, ensuring easy water drainage. In some areas, coffee plants grow under the shade of tall trees, while in others, they thrive directly under the sun, benefiting from cooler temperatures due to the altitude. The cherries are processed using the washed method, which means fermentation takes place after the coffee fruit is pulped, and it is then dried, typically in the sun.

Upon roasting, Yirgacheffe yields a coffee with a light body and pronounced acidity. The aroma is of remarkable complexity: abundant tropical fruity, and citrusy notes (especially coconut and mandarin) are complemented by undertones of toasted bread, biscuit, chocolate, and occasionally, hazelnut.

ETHIOPIAN SIDAMO

This exceptional quality coffee traces its roots to the birthplace of coffee, situated less than 100 miles (150 kilometers) from Kaffa, within the region inhabited by the Sidama people.

These coffee plantations thrive at an elevation of 5,900 feet (1,800 meters) above sea level on fertile volcanic uplands. The climate in this region is characterized by temperatures ranging around 81 °F (27 °C). Rainfall is primarily concentrated between February and April, with an annual average ranging from 1.9 to 6.5 feet (600–2,000 mm). The coffee drupes, which are exclusively of the Arabica variety in this area, undergo a relatively extended ripening period, spanning from August to December. They are meticulously hand-picked one by one and processed using the wet method, resulting in the production of exquisite small gray coffee beans.

Upon tasting, this coffee unveils the distinctive qualities commonly associated with washed coffees. It possesses a delicate body, devoid of bitterness, and boasts a well-balanced acidity that contributes to its rich aroma profile. The flavor notes encompass floral undertones, hints of honey, citrus, and tropical fruits.

These notes gradually transition to subtle nuances of dried fruits, occasionally accompanied by gentle spices, and sometimes even revealing traces of wild or earthy scents that add depth and complexity to the overall experience.

GUATEMALA ANTIGUA PASTORES

Guatemala Antigua Pastores plantations were introduced by the Jesuits in the 18th century. Today, these plantations are situated between 4,900 and 5,900 feet (1,500–1,800 meters) above sea level, on slopes created by nearby volcanoes. These slopes are close to Antigua, the city known as the "city of knights" in Guatemala. During the 16th century, Antigua served as the country's capital.

This region boasts volcanic soil, enriched by the expansive trees that provide shade and coolness to the coffee plants. Here, you can find both ancient Bourbon and Typica varietals as well as the more recent Catuai. The cherries ripen between August and September. They are still often handpicked, subsequently pulped and fermented, and finally sun-dried.

Among the Guatemalan coffees, Antigua Pastores stands out as one of the finest. It's very responsive during roasting and retains a pleasant acidity. This acidity is balanced by a highly complex aroma: floral and fresh fruit notes intertwine with deeper toasted nuances, like bakery and cocoa. Additionally, there are subtle hints of licorice and anise.

HAITIAN BLUE PINE FOREST

This quality originates from the southeastern region of Haiti's island, specifically Thiotte, which is the most renowned for coffee production. The average temperature stands at 77°F (25°C). The dry season runs from November to May, succeeded by the rainy season. The significant temperature variation between day and night contributes to the development of valuable aroma precursors in the beans. The plantations, primarily consisting of the Typica variety, thrive on clayey soils at altitudes reaching up to 5,200 feet (1,600 meters) above sea level. The cherries are processed using the wet method and are expertly roasted. Upon tasting, the coffee reveals distinct pastry notes, such as caramel and biscuits, complemented by hints of dried fruit, especially almond.

HAWAII KONA

There are five volcanoes in Hawaii, and two of them, Hualalai and Mauna Loa, offer soil that's particularly conducive to coffee cultivation. This is especially true on the island's western side, where the climate is drier – receiving less than one foot of rainfall, or just a few hundred millimeters, annually. The average temperature hovers around 77°F (25°C), with minimal fluctuations throughout the year. The soil, birthed from basaltic lava, hosts Arabica plants that grow in holes carved into the rock. These plants start to flourish in February, bearing the first fruits from August to the following January. After harvest, the coffee undergoes the wet processing method: the cherries are pulped, and the beans are left to ferment for 36–48 hours. They are then spread out on "hoshidana" covered drying decks for one to two weeks. After meticulous roasting, these beans produce a coffee with a distinct clarity. It presents pronounced fresh notes – sometimes even a hint of mint – paired with the familiar undertones of caramel, malt, dried fruit, and occasionally, pepper.

INDIAN MYSORE PLANTATION

Indian Mysore Plantation coffee has been cultivated since 1670 in the region bearing the same name, located in the southwestern part of the peninsula. This area spans between the Kodagu mountain region and the Karnataka region. The annual rainfall here fluctuates between 5.7 and 7.2 feet (1750–2200 millimeters), though in certain years it can surge up to 9.8 feet (3000 millimeters), with rains primarily in July, August, and November. The average temperature stands at 59°F (15°C), dipping to lows of 52°F (11°C) and climbing to highs of 83°F (28°C) between April and May.

The coffee plantations, situated at elevations ranging from 3200 to 4900 feet (1000–1500 meters) above sea level, predominantly feature Cauvery coffee. This variety is closely related to Catimor – an Arabica strain – that thrives under the canopy of tall trees. The harvest of the coffee cherries occurs from October to February, yielding roughly 6600 lbs (3000 kilograms) per hectare. Post-harvest, these cherries undergo wet processing. Once dried, the beans are meticulously sorted. Upon tasting, this coffee showcases a light body, punctuated with unique aromatic notes reminiscent of pastries and spices.

JAMAICAN BLUE MOUNTAIN

This coffee is named after the towering Jamaican mountains that ascend to 8,047 feet (2,453 meters) above sea level. This region encompasses multiple microclimate zones, marked by copious rainfall (ranging from 16 to 22 feet or 5,000 to 7,000 mm annually) and fertile volcanic soils, abundantly enriched with nitrogen, phosphorus, potassium, and an impressive assortment of microelements.

The "Blue Mountain" label specifically designates the Typica Arabica crops from the areas of St. Thomas, St. Andrew, and Portland. The growth cycle for this coffee is notably slow, with cherries taking up to ten months to mature fully. Harvested by hand during the summer (through August), these cherries undergo wet processing, subsequently being pulped, dried, and fermented for an extended duration (sometimes exceeding a month). They are dried with meticulous care. Uniquely, this coffee is stored and sold in white oak barrels, setting it apart from the conventional coffees typically packaged in jute bags.

Blue Mountain is a highly acclaimed coffee, and some assert it's the world's most well-rounded variety. Though it exhibits a notable acidity, when roasted properly, it adopts a silky texture, accentuating flavors of candied citrus fruits, almond, vanilla, chocolate, and hints of tobacco.

KENYA AA

On the terraced, acidic, volcanic soils around Mount Kenya, Arabica plantations thrive at elevations ranging from 4,200 to 6,800 feet (1,300–2,100 meters) above sea level. Sheltered under tall banana trees, the coffee cherries mature for the initial harvest between June and August, with the primary harvest unfolding between October and December.

Utilizing the wet process, the skin and pulp of the cherries are removed, and the beans are subsequently laid out to dry either on cement slabs or directly on farmyard grounds.

Kenyan coffee, often labeled "AA" to indicate its large bean size, stands as one of the world's most citrusy and floral coffees. Occasionally, one might even discern a hint of rose. Distinctly acidic, this coffee's profile is rounded out by notes of green apple and other fresh fruits.

KOPI LUWAK

In Java, Sumatra, and Sulawesi, a small mammal resides – the Asian palm civet. Known in Indonesia as the "Luwak" (Paradoxurus hermaphroditus), it has a particular fondness for coffee cherries. This creature is notably selective, preferring only the ripest cherries which provide a rich source of energy (given the pulp can contain up to 25% sugar), vitamins, and minerals. As the cherries pass through the civet's digestive system, most of the fruit is processed, leaving the seeds – laden with active olfactory compounds – to be expelled in the feces. Locals gather these excretions, drying them to extract and further dry the beans, which are then used to produce one of the world's most sought-after coffee varieties.

The aforementioned islands cultivate both Arabica and Robusta coffee, with the type dependent on the plantation's elevation.

While its rarity has skyrocketed its fame, this coffee bears a slightly bitter taste, punctuated by a robust aroma with evident dry fruit undertones (often hazelnut). Nuances of pastry and spices accompany a subtle hint of the very medium in which the beans were found. However, the quality of this coffee doesn't always justify its hefty price tag. The current practices of farming these civets and force-feeding them for mass production have made this coffee's production a topic of controversy.

MEXICO COATEPEC

This coffee hails from the Coatepec region of Mexico, marked by its notably rainy climate – averaging 6.2 feet (or 1900 millimeters) of precipitation annually – especially from June through September. Temperatures in the region fluctuate between 48 °F and 86 °F (9–30 °C). The coffee plantations are nestled between elevations of 4200 to 4900 feet (1300–1500 meters) above sea level. The soil varies widely; some plots are rich in organic material, while others teem with minerals. Predominant in this region are two Arabica varietals: Typica and Flat. These high-altitude coffee plants flourish under the shade of towering trees, neighbored by a plethora of medicinal herbs that play a vital role in preventing erosion. The coffee harvest spans from November to January. Following careful selection, the beans are sun-dried in accordance with the dry method.

Once properly roasted, these beans yield a coffee that is full-bodied and low in acidity. Its aromatic profile boasts clear notes of dried fruit, toasted bread, and chocolate, occasionally enhanced with a hint of spice, like pepper.

MEXICO MARAGOGYPE

In Northern Chiapas, a dry region where temperatures range between 59 °F and 95 °F (15–35 °C), coffee plants thrive at altitudes of 2600 to 4500 feet (800–1400 meters) above sea level. Among these is one of the world's largest coffee beans: a variant of Typica known as Maragogype. This Arabica variety can produce seeds that are, at times, double or even triple the average size of a typical coffee bean.

Noted for its low caffeine content, this coffee has a slightly bitter and refreshing taste. Its aromatic profile boasts notes of apple, banana, honey, chocolate, tea, and tobacco.

MONSOONED MALABAR

This coffee hails from India, cultivated in plantations situated between 3600 and 3900 feet (1100–1200 meters) above sea level. The region experiences average temperatures ranging from 77 °F to 83 °F (25–28 °C) and sees abundant rainfall, reaching up to 6.5 feet (2,000 millimeters) annually between June and November. In this environment, the Kent and Catuai drupes mature between November and February. Once harvested and dried, these fruits are exposed to the monsoon winds for a span of three to four months, lending this coffee its distinctive character.

The practice of exposing beans to monsoon winds originates from observations made on coffee beans transported from India to Europe via the Cape of Good Hope. During this journey, the beans would undergo a transformation: shifting from green to yellow in hue and, upon roasting, revealing a balanced profile with a uniquely captivating aroma. This process was then intentionally replicated on land by subjecting the beans to the damp winds blowing along the Malabar coast.

Monsooned Malabar coffee, especially when brewed as an espresso, boasts a robust body complemented by low acidity and an aromatic profile dominated by notes of dried fruit, chocolate, and spices. However, in instances where fermentation is not entirely successful, one might detect musty undertones reminiscent of dairy products.

NEPAL MOUNT EVEREST SUPREME

Mount Everest is not only the world's highest mountain, but it's also one of the rare locales north of the Tropic of Cancer where coffee cherries mature. In the Nuwakot region, at the foothills of the Ganesh Himal mountains, lies a monsoon-affected area. From June to August, this region, situated between 6500 and 7800 feet (2000–2400 meters) above sea level, experiences both rain and wind. Here, the Caturra Arabica coffee plantations thrive. Between November and January, they yield ripe, dark red cherries brimming with aromatic compounds. Processed using the wet method and then expertly roasted, the beans produce a coffee with a rounded, slightly bitter taste. It has minimal acidity and a rich aromatic profile, showcasing notes of citrus, ginger, cinnamon, cocoa, tobacco, and almond. Due to these attributes, Nepal Mount Everest Supreme has earned the moniker "the meditation coffee."

PUERTO RICO YAUCO SELECTO

This coffee hails from the Caribbean, specifically from the smallest island of the Greater Antilles: Puerto Rico. Coffee was introduced to Puerto Rico in 1736 from Martinique. Thirty years later, the city of Yauco was founded and quickly earned a reputation as the premier coffee city.

The coffee plantations benefit from a lengthy rainy season, which lasts from October to February, and they flourish in the island's predominantly volcanic, fertile soil. Once ripe, the Bourbon drupes are hand-picked, undergo the wet processing method, and are then sun-dried.

While coffee from Puerto Rico is already highly esteemed, the Puerto Rico Yauco Selecto, which makes up a mere 1% of the island's total coffee production, is especially sought after. When properly roasted, this coffee justifies its price, delighting aficionados with its robust body, refreshing taste, minimal bitterness, and a deep aromatic bouquet. Its notes span dry and fresh fruits, grains, baked goods, and occasionally, a distinct hint of peanut.

SAINT HELENA

Saint Helena boasts one of the world's most exclusive coffees. This renowned coffee hails from the eponymous island situated midway between Africa and America, famously known as Napoleon's place of exile. Despite its subtropical climate, the island has a distinct weather pattern: the Trade Winds influence temperatures on the coast, which fluctuate between 58°F and 90°F (14–32°C). These temperatures drop further inland. The island receives modest annual rainfall, capping at about 3.2 feet (1000 mm).

The coffee plantations, primarily comprising Bourbon plants, are situated approximately 2,200 feet (700 meters) above sea level. They thrive in the island's fertile volcanic soil, further enriched by guano – bird droppings. Large trees shield the Coffea Arabica shrubs from the sun and wind. However, the output from these plants is relatively low. The drupes undergo two harvests a year. Processed using the wet method, they are then dried for an extended period, sometimes spanning several months.

The outcome is truly exceptional. Some coffee aficionados even claim that Saint Helena produces the world's finest coffee. This coffee's sensory profile boasts a pleasing acidity paired with floral and fruity undertones. Intriguing hints of citrus are followed by toasted bread, baked goods, and dried fruit nuances.

WHERE IS COFFEE CULTIVATED AND HOW

GIANT SALVADOR PACAMARA

The Maragogype, an exceptional varietal of the Bourbon that originated in Brazil, paved the way for the Pacamara in the small state of El Salvador along the Pacific Ocean. Like its progenitor, the Pacamara boasts impressively large beans. Nestled in El Salvador's volcanic mountain range with its fertile soil and ample rainfall – exceeding 6.5 feet (2000 millimeters) annually from May to October – the Pacamara thrives. Its cycle culminates in the ripening of the fruits between January and May.

While the yield per hectare is somewhat modest, the outcome in the cup is nothing short of delightful. The coffee delivers a harmonious balance, marked by fresh and unexpected herbal undertones such as tea and tobacco. These flavors are further enhanced by hints of spice, notably licorice, and toasted pastry.

SULAWESI KOPI TORAJA TONGKONAN

The island of Sulawesi, situated in Indonesia, boasts a tropical climate, maintaining an average temperature of 86 °F (30 °C) throughout the year. A dry spell spans from May to August, while rains dominate from November to March. Given its mountainous terrain, the island has a variety of distinct microclimates. Coffee plantations flourish at altitudes between 4200 and 6500 feet (1300–2000 meters) above sea level, rooted in volcanic soil. Given that some of the island's volcanoes remain active, the soil is rich in minerals, advantageous for the coffee plants sheltered beneath tall trees. The primary variety grown here is the Jember, also recognized as Kopy Jember or S795, a hybrid resulting from the natural cross-breeding of Arabica and Liberica with Kent. Notably, this variety yields sparsely (3300 lbs/1500 kilograms per hectare). Its plants can tower up to 19 feet (6 meters) and have a lifespan of around fifty years.

Of particular interest is the traditional processing technique used for this coffee: a variant of the wet method where the drupes undergo fermentation in small barrels, followed by an extended drying phase, sometimes lasting up to a month, due to challenging weather conditions. The result is one of the world's most sought-after coffees. Its exclusivity is attributed to its limited production, meticulous selection process, unique barrel storage, and distinct sensory characteristics. Though washed, this coffee boasts a robust body and moderate acidity. Its aromatic profile is marked by balsamic notes and spices, harmoniously intertwined with fresh and dried fruit flavors.

WHERE IS COFFEE CULTIVATED AND HOW

HOW IS COFFEE CULTIVATED?

The propagation of the coffee plant can take place through sowing or cutting. The first method entails collecting ripe fruits, selecting the best seeds, and placing them in wooden boxes filled with soil and humus to await the growth of new seedlings. In the second method, a branch is taken from a mature plant and planted directly into the soil. These future coffee plants are placed in a nursery where they stay for about a year before being transferred to the main plantations. There, after roughly three years, they begin to produce. Interestingly, the coffee plant's life cycle and fruit-bearing timeline are similar to that of the vine. On average, a coffee plantation remains productive for about twenty years. However, there are exceptions. In some regions, coffee plants can live for up to half a century, and there are even individual plants that have survived for over a century.

The choice between propagation by seed or cutting depends on the goals. While the first method is more straightforward, the second ensures that the offspring retain the characteristics of the parent plant. It's important to note that with seeds, it's difficult to predict the exact genetic makeup that will result from a fertilized flower. This unpredictability can lead to natural mutations and hybrids, or those that arise through human intervention.

A coffee plantation inspection in the Orosi River Valley in Costa Rica.

THE PLANTATION

The environments suitable for coffee cultivation can vary greatly in terms of orography (like land elevations and slopes), soil type (ranging from volcanic to Brazil's red soil), rainfall, and exposure to wind and sun. Coffee plants might thrive under the shelter of tall, shady trees or even in direct sunlight. Another environmental consideration is the presence of pests and diseases that can threaten a plantation's yield and even its survival. The collective environmental attributes of a specific region heavily influence the choice of coffee species and variety, as well as the cultivation techniques employed.

Regarding soil, coffee plants favor light, well-draining soils enriched with humus, nitrogen, potassium, and phosphorus. Nitrogen primarily fuels the growth of the trunk and leaves. Potassium plays a crucial role in producing sugar-rich drupes – and importantly, the higher the sugar concentration, the more aromatic the roasted beans become. Phosphorus is vital for flowering and, subsequently, drupe production. It's also worth noting that while coffee plants enjoy shade, they rely on light as their primary energy source for cellulose synthesis, which facilitates growth. Consequently, the plant's exposure – which ties in with factors like wind, transpiration, and pollination – is of utmost importance.

Annual rainfall is crucial, both in terms of quantity and distribution. While superior plants living beyond the tropics base their cycles on seasons – marked by temperature shifts and sun exposure – coffee plants revolve their cycles around rain, blooming after every rainfall.

Equally significant is the interplay between latitude and altitude in shaping the climate. As one

The incredible geometries of a Brazilian plantation.

WHERE IS COFFEE CULTIVATED AND HOW

WHERE IS COFFEE CULTIVATED AND HOW

moves away from the equator, average temperatures drop and slopes generally become gentler. Consider the Brazilian hills of Mogiana and Minas where coffee plants grow at lower altitudes (with Arabica situated around 1,600 feet or 500 meters above sea level), bathed in direct sunlight, in neat, low rows – reminiscent of vineyards. These conditions allow for mechanical harvesting. However, limited water availability means that these regions cannot produce washed coffees that demand the "wet" method. Conversely, nearer to the equator, temperatures rise. To find the optimal climate, coffee must seek higher elevations, even up to 9,100 feet (2,800 meters) above sea level. Here, the sun's intensity requires that coffee plants grow under the canopy of tall trees, on precipitous terrains with uneven soils. These conditions preclude mechanical harvesting. Yet, abundant water resources enable the production of premium washed coffee.

Altitude also influences the density of the coffee cherries, an attribute closely tied to the fruit's sugar content. This has led to a distinction between hard beans and soft beans. The boundary separating these two categories is conventionally drawn at around 4,900 feet (1,500 meters) above sea level. However, as mentioned earlier, the placement of this demarcation is greatly influenced by factors like latitude, exposure, plantation type, and certainly the specific coffee species and variety.

A crucial determinant in assessing coffee quality is the thermal excursion, which refers to the temperature variance between day and night. This fluctuation influences the development of terpenic precursors, pivotal in endowing coffee with floral and balsamic nuances when brewed. While this charac-

Rows of coffee trees on the Hawaiian island of Kauai.

teristic is predominantly observed in high-altitude washed coffees, it is intriguingly present in certain natural coffees – those processed using the dry method – that grow at lesser altitudes in regions experiencing significant temperature excursions during the coffee cherry ripening phase.

Furthermore, environmental factors markedly affect the synthesis of caffeine and phenolic acids. Caffeine, an alkaloid, bestows coffee with its cherished psychotropic attributes. However, when present in high concentrations, it can restrict the beverage's consumption. To put it simply: while coffee should be a delightful experience, elevated caffeine levels necessitate moderate consumption. Phenolic acids, ubiquitous in all plants, can introduce an off-putting sensation called astringency (akin to biting into an unripe persimmon) when they exceed certain levels or are of specific types.

These compounds – caffeine and phenolic acids – serve as vital defenses for the coffee plant. Consequently, when coffee is grown under conditions where defense mechanisms are less required, such as against pests, the plant tends to produce fewer of these molecules. Altitude plays a role here: higher elevations naturally reduce threats like pests. Thus, Robusta coffee cultivated at higher altitudes is slightly less "Robusta" in character, while Arabica grown at lower elevations displays a touch more of the "Robusta" trait.

LIFE CYCLE OF THE COFFEE PLANT

In temperate regions, plants bloom in spring, heralded by rising temperatures signaling winter's end. However, in tropical climates, rain triggers the flowering process.

After each rainfall, the coffee plant bears its delicate white flowers. Once pollinated, these flowers yield what botanists refer to as drupes, but which are commonly known as coffee cherries. Depending on the environment, a coffee plant might experience a single wet season followed by a dry one, or it might endure a singular season marked by sporadic rainfalls interspersed with dry spells. In the latter scenario, a single coffee plant might simultaneously showcase flowers, recently pollinated fruits, maturing drupes, and cherries ready for harvesting. Consequently, unlike the grape harvest, which typically spans just a couple of months, some regions might witness a coffee harvest that extends throughout most of the year, or even twice within a year. This variability implies that the duration from flower pollination to drupe ripening can fluctuate significantly – anywhere from six to ten months – contingent upon the location.

Regardless of the location, post-pollination, the ovary starts to expand, resulting in the formation of the drupe. Initially green, the drupe transitions to a bright red hue, and eventually to a near-brown shade. However, there are instances of orange-hued drupes, much like how grapes' appearances vary based on their variety.

THE FRUIT

The coffee fruit is a drupe, meaning it's fleshy. It consists of a thin exocarp (skin), a juicy and sugary sarcocarp (pulp), a fine, fibrous endocarp (parchment), a silvery film, and typically two seeds that lie flat against each other. Generally, there are two seeds, but occasionally, due to the abortion of one of the two seeds, the space is taken up by a singular bean. This unique bean produces a distinct type of coffee known as "caracolito."

The appearance of the seeds can distinguish different coffee species: Arabica beans have an S-shaped crack running down the middle of the flat side, while Robusta beans feature a straight line. In general, Robusta seeds are smaller and rounder, whereas Arabica seeds are larger and more elliptical.

While coffee drupes are smaller than more familiar drupes like cherries, and despite their rich content of sugars and organic acids, they often go unused. In fact, they sometimes pose an environmental cost. What's valuable to humans are the two seeds inside. These seeds can vary in size – only a few millimeters in some species and over a centimeter in others, such as the Maragogype. It takes about fifty of these beans to brew a single cup of coffee. Given that coffee shrubs aren't typical garden plants, let's delve into how these beans are processed to produce coffee.

48-49 Red coffee drupes in Brazil.

50-51 Coffee harvest in Zambia.

WHERE IS COFFEE CULTIVATED AND HOW

HARVESTING TECHNIQUES: PICKING, STRIPPING, AND MECHANICAL HARVESTING

Once ripe, the coffee fruit is plucked from the plant. There are three primary methods to accomplish this. The first is known as coffee picking. In this method, the drupes are handpicked individually, much like cherries. Although the skin of the coffee fruit is quite tough, it can still get damaged, leading the fruit to begin to decay. This decay can result in the final beverage having an unpleasant, putrid flavor, akin to the scent you'd encounter near a garbage heap. The riper the fruit, the more fragile it is. Hence, the over-ripe fruits needed to produce some of the highest quality coffees are exceptionally delicate. In such situations, manual coffee picking proves optimal, even if it's the priciest option.

A more cost-effective manual method is stripping. With this method, one holds the coffee branch in one hand and uses the other to strip away all its drupes, allowing them to fall into containers (like aprons or baskets) placed beneath.

52-53 On this plantation in Thailand, ripe coffee drupes are handpicked one by one.

54-55 A great harvest at a coffee plantation in Ethiopia.

This method is quicker, but it often results in the collection of many leaves along with the drupes. Moreover, it doesn't allow for distinguishing between varying levels of ripeness. Thus, stripping is best suited for coffee varieties grown in regions where the fruits ripen simultaneously.

The third method is mechanical harvesting: large machines traverse the plantation rows, shaking the coffee plants to make the fruit fall into a collection hopper. Naturally, this method is only viable where the terrain and the configuration of the plantation permit it, such as in expansive plantations and in *fazendas* where the beans can be sorted based on their ripeness.

Regardless of the collection method, the ripeness of the beans is pivotal for several reasons:

- Ripe fruits contain fewer phenolic acids, which can cause astringency, and reduced levels of malic acid. The presence of malic acid, which isn't significantly diminished during roasting, can give the brew a notably unpleasant sharpness in taste.

- As the fruits ripen, their pyrazine levels drop. Pyrazine is responsible for the pronounced herbaceous notes and ashy flavor in roasted beans.

- In fully ripe drupes, the sugar concentration can reach 23-25%. This high sugar content is vital for achieving a pronounced aromatic intensity during roasting.

THE EXTRACTION OF THE BEANS

Though the coffee drupe doesn't possess a substantial amount of pulp, this pulp still accounts for a significant portion of the whole fruit. It must be removed, along with the skin, to access the coffee beans.

The most ancient method, referred to as the "dry" method which yields the so-called "natural" coffees, predominantly relies on the sun: the drupes are spread out on the farmyard ground (nowadays, this is typically a tiled surface to prevent unwanted contaminants that might influence the final outcome). Here, the drupes are left to dry, gradually losing their moisture. The pulp and skin become less supple, dry out, and can then be effortlessly stripped away, leaving the coffee bean still enveloped in its chaff (or silver-skin).

The conditions under which this transition occurs – particularly its duration – critically influence the development of aroma precursors. These precursors will later manifest during the roasting process and in the finished beverage. Natural coffees are vital for achieving a brew with a robust body and subdued acidity, offering chocolate undertones and occasionally hints of spices, notably pepper.

57 Coffee drying in the sun in Nicaragua.

*58-59 Thanks to meticulous and incessant work, the coffee harvest of this southern
Indian plantation can be left to dry in the sun.*

WHERE IS COFFEE CULTIVATED AND HOW

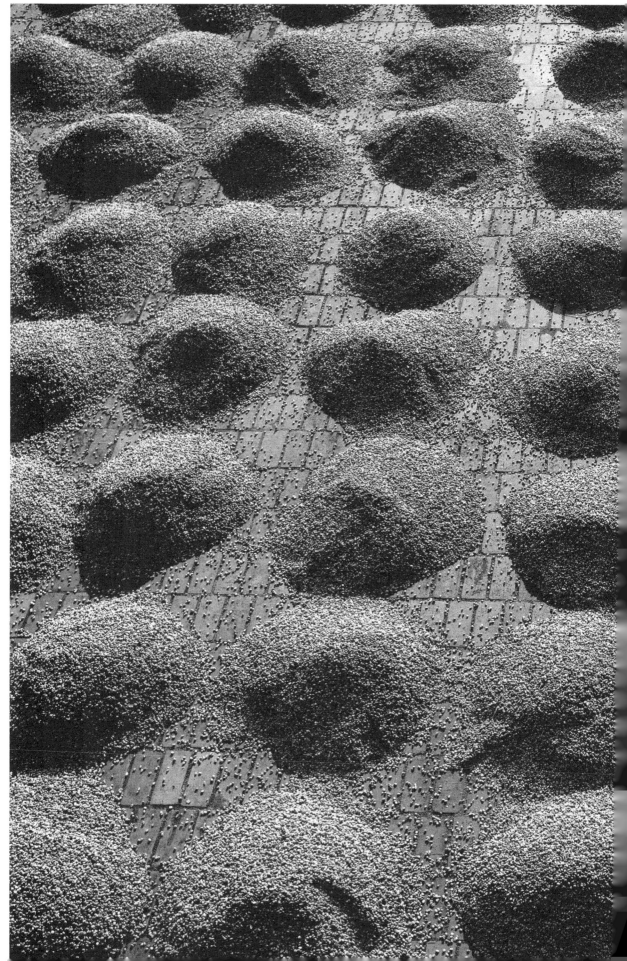

Although this method doesn't amplify the floral accents, when the coffee originates from areas with pronounced temperature fluctuations, there can be hints of floral and refined balsamic notes. These are distinct from the crude green notes characteristic of underripe beans.

The second approach is the so-called "wet processing," which produces "washed coffees." Although the traditional wet method persists in certain regions, this technique is comparatively modern because it demands machinery capable of stripping away the skin and pulp, leaving only the beans encased in a sugary, sticky film. Historically, this process involved the use of mortars and pestles, but over time, increasingly efficient machines were developed. To separate the coffee beans from their outer coatings, the fruits are submerged in water to ferment. Within this watery environment, the largely spontaneous – and thus challenging to regulate – actions of myriad microorganisms commence. Predominantly yeasts and bacteria dominate this process, as molds are inhibited by the relatively high acidity levels. These microorganisms consume the residual sugars and release a surge of enzymes that target the outer layers, leaving only the beans. Once freed from their outer layers, the beans are then prepared for drying. This can be under the sun or in shade, often laid out on mats elevated slightly above the ground. They are spread in thin layers and consistently turned and shuffled, then covered during the nighttime. In certain instances, these drying platforms also have roofs to shield the beans from direct sun exposure.

Guatemala: coffee drupes being washed to separate the precious seeds from the pulp.

WHERE IS COFFEE CULTIVATED AND HOW

Washed coffees are typically produced in regions with abundant water and an affordable labor force, as this process is often reserved for cherries collected using the picking method. However, beans that undergo wet processing yield superior coffee flavors. They present fresh acidic notes and are rarely bitter or astringent. Their aromatic profile is broad, encompassing notes of honey, floral scents (including hints of roses), tropical and citrus fruits, stone fruits like peaches and apricots, and dried fruits, with walnut being especially prominent.

The third method, which is relatively recent, yields the semi-washed coffees. This procedure came into use once pulping machines attained such high levels of efficiency that they could perfectly clean the beans, making them ready for drying. Beans processed with this method provide a coffee with characteristics that fall between those obtained with the two older processes. However, in reality, they share little in common with fully-washed coffees, given that they haven't undergone the fermentation process.

In the preparation of green coffee (this is what coffee is termed before being roasted), it's essential to understand that most producers typically aim for safe and consistent production. This goal has often been achieved, sometimes at the expense of top-quality results. In other words: while most coffees are good, very few are exceptional. A significant tool aiding this objective is the drying oven. While it certainly prevents harmful fermentations, it shortens the process so much that the bean doesn't experience the necessary breakdown of crucial elements, and there isn't ample time for the formation of beneficial enzymes. The use of a drying oven also negates the need for sun-drying the beans, an action that many experts believe plays a pivotal role in the development of aroma precursors.

SELECTION, CLASSIFICATION AND PACKAGING

Based on the overall quality of a production, the drupes might undergo varying levels of selection. However, when it comes to beans, selection is absolutely critical. This bean selection can either be done manually by workers who can't handle heavy labor (often youths, women, and older individuals) or by machines. These machines gauge the color of the beans as they pass, one by one, in front of a light beam. The primary aim of this operation is to weed out any defective beans to meet product classification standards. But with the introduction of mechanical harvesting, the selection process has become even more vital to prevent the inclusion of unripe beans, which can greatly degrade the quality of the brewed coffee.

Another classification hinges on the size of the beans. They are sorted by sifting them through screens with holes of specific sizes. The most sought-after coffee beans are of size 17/18, while smaller ones are often deemed less valuable. However, this isn't always indicative of their sensory properties. That said, batches of coffee beans of uniform size do ensure a much-improved roasting process.

Cupping, or the sensory evaluation of coffee, is paramount. In coffee-producing regions, there are professional coffee tasters who might sample up to 300 coffees daily. These are all prepared using the Brazilian method: infusing ground coffee in hot water. While this method is suitable for tasting, it doesn't suffice for certain specific coffee preparations, such as Italian espresso.

Once the coffee is selected and classified, it's ready for packaging. Typically, the beans are stored in 132-lb (60-kg) jute bags (with very few deviations from this size). These bags often bear the name of the producer and/or the coffee's origin. Alternatively, some coffee is stored in larger containers, or in the case of particularly high-quality varieties, small wooden barrels.

64-65 Workers controlling and selecting coffee drupes on a southern Indian plantation.

ROASTING

FROM PERFORATED ROASTING PANS TO FLUID BED ROASTERS

The discovery of fire by humankind not only improved the hygienic qualities of food but also enhanced its sensory characteristics, heightening pleasure. This pivotal discovery soon influenced the consumption of coffee, transitioning from boiling drupes to infusing expertly roasted beans.

As we've observed, the coffee drupe has a sugary pulp. Yet, unlike other fruits, humans haven't shown a strong preference for them. These drupes lack an enticing aroma, with a dominant, persistent green note, and their sweetness in taste is often overshadowed by a distinct acidity, frequently paired with astringency. A decoction made from coffee drupes likely wasn't particularly appealing. Had our ancestors settled for that, coffee might not have achieved its global popularity.

Even raw beans carry a herby flavor, leading them to be termed "green coffee." However, when appropriately roasted, they emit an irresistibly rich aroma. Some claim that a cup of brewed coffee contains double the number of molecules found in wine. This might be an exaggeration, but it's undeniable that roasting significantly amplifies these molecules. In fact, over 1,500 such molecules have been identified in the final coffee product using current technologies. And as technology progresses, who knows how many more we might detect in the future? Intriguingly, our sense of smell can perceive certain notes that even the most advanced equipment might overlook, and some of these notes possess an almost subliminal allure.

It's possible that the aroma of molecules wafting from coffee plants during a fire captivated the senses of our ancestors. Alternatively, and perhaps more likely, coffee might have been just another ingredient that early humans experimented with after discovering fire. The specifics remain elusive. However, what is clear is that the discovery of roasted coffee beans significantly influenced the trajectory of human history.

For centuries, this breakthrough delineated humanity into two primary cultures: one that indulged in fermented beverages like wine and beer, and another that drew vitality from the stimulating power of coffee.

We can't be certain about the design of the earliest roasting equipment, but it likely resembled a terracotta vessel. However, baked clay – or its refined version, ceramic – doesn't conduct heat as efficiently as metal, a material whose discovery probably predates that of roasted coffee. Regardless of whether these vessels were made of terracotta or metal, it's plausible that they had perforations, allowing some degree of direct contact between the flame and the beans. As a result, the early coffee might have carried hints of roasted chestnuts in its flavor profile. This could have set the precedent for the perforated roasting pans still in use today. Ancient roasting pans might have started as basic pans, with the subsequent addition of a lidded handle to constantly stir the beans over the flame.

In this scenario – and continuing until the late 19th century – the roasting method relied primarily on conduction, essentially delivering heat through a medium, such as iron. While this method achieved the fundamental goal, the aroma of the coffee was sometimes marred by burnt undertones, and its taste marred by an unpalatable mix of bitter and sour notes. The utilization of hollow steel spheres, which rotated over a heat source (typically burning wood), enhanced the roasting outcome by ensuring more uniform heating. Eventually, wood gave way to coal, a fuel that allowed for finer heat regulation, thus paving the way for further advancements. However, the true breakthrough in roasting quality emerged post-World War II with the introduction of gas-heated roasters, where heat was primarily delivered through convection, using hot air.

But before diving deeper into these advancements, it's essential to address two other crucial aspects of the roasting process: smoke and cooling. Roasting coffee invariably produces smoke, separate from the

fumes created by the heat source. As professional coffee roasting enterprises began to process larger quantities in the early 20th century, smoke extractors were incorporated to direct the smoke outdoors.

Around the same time, there arose a need to address the slow cooling of beans. Once coffee beans attain a certain roast level, they begin to emit heat instead of absorbing it. Consequently, the beans continue to roast even after being removed from the heat source. This can severely jeopardize quality, particularly when roasting large quantities. With home roasting – still prevalent in some countries like Japan where green coffee is sold at local markets – the quantities are obviously smaller, and simply placing the beans on a cold surface suffices to halt the roasting process. In early commercial roasting setups, beans were poured onto elevated static grids, where they were continually turned to expedite cooling. Later came the invention of forced air cooling basins. The most recent innovation involves the use of nitrogen for cooling, leveraging its ability to rapidly chill the air. However, amidst these effective strategies, some attempted to take shortcuts by dousing the roasted beans with water for quicker cooling: undoubtedly one of the surest ways to impair the coffee's aroma and reduce its longevity.

Let's revisit the evolution of roasting techniques. Wood, still utilized in Brazil and by artisans globally, was gradually supplanted in some cases by coal, followed by diesel, and finally gas. As a result, roasting shifted from being driven by conduction to convection, profoundly influencing the end product. In this context, it's essential to highlight a groundbreaking advancement from the last quarter of the century: the incorporation of clean air to channel heat.

However, innovation wasn't limited to drum coffee roasters. Beans have been roasted using irradiation (specifically, microwaves), in Archimedean screw-pump machines that thrust the beans into a stream of hot air, and even in fluid bed roasters. In the latter method, green beans enter a high-temperature air cyclone. As they fall, the beans roast, lose weight, start floating, and are ultimately ejected from the top.

ROASTING TECHNIQUES

For many years, roasters followed a consistent design: a rotating cylinder filled with coffee beans that were exposed to hot air. These drum roasters, enduring for centuries, could last several lifetimes and had capacities ranging from a few pounds to several hundred. Industry professionals often argue that the prime roasters have capacities between 132 to 264 lbs (60–120 kilograms). Still, outstanding coffee can be roasted in machines designed for 33 or 771 lbs (15 and 350 kg). However, large-scale processing can present challenges, while smaller batches have their unique set of rules.

Nevertheless, Italian Espresso coffee, universally regarded as one of the most demanding preparations, relies on beans roasted in these drum machines. They operate in "cooking batches", encompassing a loading phase, a toasting phase, and a discharge. The cycles last between 15 and 25 minutes, the essential duration for complete aroma development, and operate at temperatures ranging from 185 °F to 419 °F (85–215 °C). Modern roasters come equipped with advanced software that streamlines and enhances safety during the process. However, constant supervision is crucial to achieve the finest roasted beans.

From the discussion so far, it's evident that the primary and critical decision is the selection of the green coffee beans. This selection process is intricate, challenging, and fraught with potential pitfalls. It's predomi-

70 and 71 Four different levels of roasting.

nantly an intuitive choice, heavily reliant on a professional's olfactory senses and experience. The decision often begins by placing a specific quantity of coffee into drum roasters, typically with capacities ranging from 0.2 to 2.2 lbs (100 grams to one kilo), and roasting it to the desired level. However, this initial step can lead to significant errors. Typically, the results from small-scale roasting do not reflect what would be achieved on a larger, industrial scale. As we will further explore, the heat generated by the bulk of coffee beans, especially when transitioning from the endothermic to the exothermic phase, is influenced by the size of the batch. But this relationship isn't straightforward or linear.

WHAT HAPPENS DURING THE ROASTING PROCESS

Inside the roaster, the beans undergo a transformation, behaving like chemical reactors. The process can be broadly categorized into two phases: endothermic and exothermic.

During the endothermic phase, the beans absorb heat from the external environment. This heat spreads throughout the bean by conduction, propelled by the transport of water vapor and carbon dioxide. As the bean loses moisture, its color changes from green to a pale yellow, and the aroma transitions from a fresh green scent to that reminiscent of baked bread. This phase sees the onset of sugar hydrolysis, giving rise to the Maillard reaction, the cornerstone of the roasting process. As the coffee reaches its zenith in the endothermic stage, the color deepens further and the beans start to expand, driven by the formation of internal gases.

The exothermic phase quickly ensues. Here, the bean's constituents generate heat, initiating what could be termed as internal combustion. If not halted timely, this could destroy the coffee beans. In this phase, there's a pronounced increase in volume due to the emergence of micro-pores and superficial micro-cracks. The beans turn fragile, and a potent aroma emerges. The pyrolytic reactions intensify, leading to significant gas release, and the beans acquire their final distinct character.

Emerging from the roaster are profoundly transformed beans. They've increased in volume by about 60%, lost most of their moisture, and their sugar content has diminished significantly. Particularly in unwashed beans, which experience a weight reduction of about 20%, there's an increased presence of fats and nitrogen compounds. The true marvel of this process is that it converts these beans into aromatic reservoirs, encapsulated within a carbon dioxide environment. Roasting results in the basic constituents of the beans interacting

72-73 Roasted coffee being cooled.

and evolving into new chemical entities. These entities, in turn, react further, giving birth to subsequent genera-tions of compounds. As a result, even minor variations in green beans can get magnified post-roasting, turning minute imperfections into significant sensory deviations in the final product.

ROASTING METHODS

If we plot time and temperature on a four-quadrant diagram – the two variables that dictate the energy needed to roast coffee – we can identify four distinct scenarios:

- fast high-temperature roasting: This method may lead to uneven bean roasting, resulting in beans that are charred on the outside and undercooked on the inside. In terms of sensory characteristics, when coffee is prepared using the espresso method under this roasting profile, it typically lacks a creamy layer (or has very little of it that is not persistent and lacks texture). The balance between bitterness and acidity is disrupted, as both are quite strong. The coffee tends to be lacking in body and can exhibit a tendency towards astringency. It may also possess empyreumatic (smoky or burnt) aromas with limited complexity in its aroma profile.
- long high-temperature roasting: This approach results in a dark roast with intensified crema color. Astrin-gency and bitterness become more pronounced. Floral and fruity notes tend to diminish, making way for the emergence of medicinal notes, often associated with increased phenol formation. The ratio of vinyl-guaiacol to ethylguaiacol shifts in favor of the former, reducing aromatic finesse.
- long low-temperature roasting: This combination of factors leads to excessive pyridine formation, which imparts a more bitter taste and hints of cooked meat to the coffee. However, it also increases the production of thiophene, which, when exceeding certain levels, can result in onion-like aromas rather than the desired notes of honey, flowers, and toasted bread.
- short low-temperature roasting: light roast. Characterized by a light roast profile, this method results in espresso with minimal crema and texture. It lacks macromolecules, particularly due to insufficient blend-ing of proteins and sugars. As a result, the coffee has a thin body. The acidity is high, primarily due to reduced degradation of fixed aliphatic acids, contributing to a lack of harmony in the cup. Moreover, the aroma profile is limited, as there has not been sufficient formation of aromatic molecules.

REST TIME – DEGASSING

The freshly roasted coffee bean isn't ready for immediate use. It needs to undergo a "degassing" period, a phase where it releases excess gas while continuing its aromatic maturation. This process is heavily influenced by the environment: both temperature and atmospheric pressure can speed up or slow down the degassing.

There are various methods to achieve this. For medium-sized coffee roasters, it's typical to use silos. Here, the roasted coffee is stored for a few days before it's packaged. Alternatively, especially for export or long-distance shipping, the beans might be packed soon after roasting, allowing them to degas within the bags.

Regardless of the chosen method, degassing is essential. Beans that haven't been allowed to degas sufficiently produce espresso crema that's overly carbonated, resulting in a frothy, short-lived texture. Aromatically, beans that haven't adequately degassed offer a subdued aroma, as they haven't reached their full aromatic potential. However, it's crucial not to let the beans degas excessively, as this can lead to oxidation, compromising the quality.

SINGLE-ORIGIN COFFEES AND BLENDS

Each year, a significant portion of the 700 billion cups of coffee consumed worldwide is made from single-origin coffees. These are coffees sourced from a specific territory, which might be as vast as Brazil or as limited as a single plantation. As previously mentioned, in the former case, it's somewhat misleading to refer to it as "single origin". In the latter case, coffees could even be distinguished by their year of production. Similar to wine, single-origin coffee stakes its identity on its unique characteristics. When processed by a micro-roasting establishment, these qualities can yield legendary specialties. Conversely, when discussing single-origin coffee from expansive regions, while the product retains its evocative allure, its distinct traits aren't as sharply defined. This is because different batches are often mixed together to produce the final product. Although the result can technically be considered a blend, it's not a blend in the traditional sense.

In a world that predominantly lauds single-origin coffees, coffee blends respond to our deep-rooted desire for aromatic complexity. From a business perspective, a blend symbolizes a coffee roaster's signature. While the origins of various coffees might be quite similar, the roasting process and the unique combination of beans manifest the roaster's distinct flair, defining their brand.

Globally, the prowess to craft exceptional blends is a skill often linked with Italian tradition and expertise, sparking immense interest among non-Italian professionals. Indeed, an outstanding blend isn't simply the result of following a rulebook; it's the embodiment of a vision – an almost anthropological perspective, one might argue – of how diverse coffees can seamlessly meld into a singular cup. It's worth noting that the earliest blends were crafted for Italian Espresso coffee (the earliest record of this method hails from 1845). This preparation, more than any other, accentuates in the cup both the quality of the green coffee and the expertise of the roaster.

There are many types of coffee. Different coffee origins can be roasted separately and then mixed according to a precise recipe. Alternatively, green coffee beans can be mixed beforehand and then roasted.

Outlined below are the attributes essential for a blend to yield an exceptional cup of coffee:

- perfection: It should be free from visual imperfections (flawless cream), devoid of any off-putting aromas or flavors, and should offer a harmonious balance on the palate with no hint of astringency. Complementing these imperfection-free traits are a hazelnut-colored cream with tawny hints, a silky mouthfeel, an impeccable equilibrium between acidity and bitterness, and a refined, distinctive aroma.

- depth: Primarily tied to the aroma, depth pertains to the richness of positive attributes in the blend. A blend demonstrates depth when it begins with floral and fresh fruit notes, progresses to hints of dried fruit, evolves with intricate toasted undertones, and culminates in a harmonious play of spices.

- potency: This trait alludes to the blend's body and its aromatic vigor, specifically referring to the intensity and persistence of the aroma. However, potency can be detrimental if the blend lacks perfection. In essence, a coffee blend can be intensely potent even if marred by dominant undesirable aromas, astringency, or woodiness.

AXIOMS AND POSTULATES IN THE CREATION OF A BLEND

The creation of a blend is essentially an art, rooted in professional maturity, skill, knowledge, sensitivity, and passion.

This means there isn't a fixed set of rules or a guaranteed recipe one can follow to craft an excellent blend. However, there are some guiding principles one can adhere to in order to avoid major missteps:

- A good blend is built on affinities and complementarities, not on contrasts.

- The formulation of a blend abides by the rule of multiplication: hence, one negative component doesn't just coexist with the positive ones; it diminishes the entire outcome.

- Minute amounts of harmful molecules can suppress the depth of the entire blend.

HOW MANY COMPONENTS FOR A HIGH QUALITY BLEND?

The term "blend" carries distinct meanings depending on its context. In many countries, a blend simply refers to the combination of two different coffees, whether they differ by species, origin, or post-harvest processes. In Italy, however, a blend transcends its basic definition, becoming an art form deeply rooted in a specific coffee company's philosophy.

A frequently asked question centers around the ideal number of components a blend should have to produce an outstanding cup of coffee. While having only two components might seem insufficient, incorporating a multitude of components doesn't guarantee superiority.

Though there's no definitive recipe, we can propose three potential approaches:

- Complexity achieved through blending several types of coffee (ranging from 9 to 13).

- Complexity derived from a few coffee varieties that undergo diverse roasting methods.

- Complexity achieved using a handful of perfectly roasted, high-quality coffee varieties.

ROASTING SINGLE-ORIGIN COFFEES OR BLENDS

Different coffee beans from various origins can either be roasted separately and then combined in specific proportions, or they can be blended while still green and roasted together. These represent two distinct approaches, both of which are utilized worldwide, each demanding its own unique workflow and suitable equipment. Once a method is chosen, it's challenging to switch to the other. Roasting single origins individually is undeniably a strategy that highlights the beans' distinct attributes. Furthermore, this approach permits slight adjustments in the mixing ratio to refine the outcome. However, it's a more expensive method. Some coffee producers argue that roasting diverse beans together results in a richer aromatic bouquet.

Then there's the hybrid approach: blending some components before roasting and integrating the rest post-roasting.

COFFEE GRINDIN●

FROM MORTARS TO ELECTRONIC
DOSER GRINDERS

The coffee bean is truly a treasure trove. Although roasting has rendered the Coffea seed less pliable, its aroma and active molecules remain securely locked within its scarcely permeable cells. As a result, to brew a good cup of coffee, the beans must be finely ground. This allows water, usually very hot or boiling, to penetrate the coffee, extracting its rich flavors. By diminishing the bean's size, the contact surface between the water and the coffee is expanded, and the distance the solvent must traverse to reach the coffee cells is dramatically shortened. This transformation is facilitated by roasting. The heat renders the beans hard, imbuing them with a nearly glass-like brittleness. This makes the roasted beans somewhat reminiscent of coal, even in their rheological characteristics.

Once, the mortar was the sole tool at our disposal. Crafted from stone (preferably) or metal, it consisted of two pieces: the mortar and the pestle. Grinding coffee beans in a mortar is undeniably labor-intensive, but the coffee doesn't heat up, ensuring minimal aromatic loss.

Naturally, the degree of fragmentation hinges on the roast level, as well as the force and frequency of the pestle's strikes within the bowl.

In pursuit of a less primitive method, people turned to grinders, similar to those employed for spices. These were cylindrical devices equipped with mechanisms adept at pulverizing pepper grains, a spice once lauded as a cure-all and a potent aphrodisiac.

However, coffee posed a different challenge: not only are its beans considerably larger than pepper grains, but the quantities required for brewing are also more substantial.

Consequently, a more efficient tool was in demand, one that boasted a larger capacity. The answer lay in crafting a rotating mill affixed to a shaft connected to the bean container. Powered by a suitably long crank, this device could capture and shatter the beans, compelling them into the tight gap formed by the grinder's motion. These ancient grinders bore a striking resemblance to their modern counterparts, with one key distinction: they were hand-operated. Grinding coffee was typically a chore designated to children and servants.

These machines made their debut relatively late, in the seventeenth century. Their introduction was met with great enthusiasm, turning them into household status symbols: those who owned one had the privilege of savoring the exclusive coffee beverage.

The first patented model was recorded in the U.S. by Thomas Bruff in 1798. This was followed by the coffee grinder designed by British blacksmith Richard Dearman in 1799. In 1815, another Brit, Archibald Kenrick, innovated by adding a regulation screw to adjust the fineness of the grind. This proved crucial, tailoring the ground coffee to various preparation methods.

In 1818, the American Increase Wilson introduced a wall-mounted grinder design, streamlining its use for larger scale production. Meanwhile, his fellow countryman Charles Parker constructed sturdy grinders tailored for home use. With coffee consumption burgeoning, portable travel grinders equipped with foldable cranks were crafted for those on the go. The shift to industrial coffee grinding was marked by the collaboration between the French Peugeot brothers and the British Jackson brothers in 1842.

Italy embraced industrialized coffee grinding later, towards the end of the nineteenth century, spearheaded by the Tre Spade brand founded by the Bortolo brothers. The emergence of espresso coffee, a method particularly sensitive to grind size, catalyzed the evolution of renowned global brands.

Unsurprisingly, the introduction of electric motors simplified and expedited the grinding process. In the professional realm, while the fundamental mechanics remained consistent, grinders saw enhancements in construction materials, design geometry, and precision. Electronics paved the way for grinders capable of producing the exact coffee quantity needed for a cup, while also facilitating communication between the coffee maker and the grinder, optimizing their coordinated function.

However, this progress was not without missteps. The incorporation of electric motors led to the creation of electric blade grinders, a less-than-ideal invention. These machines not only heated the coffee, dissipating its aroma, but also yielded inconsistent grounds, undermining the performance of coffee machines.

COFFEE GRINDING

FROM MORTARS TO ELECTRONIC DOSER GRINDERS

Modern doser grinders made their debut in the 1920s. Before their advent, coffee was traditionally ground manually at the back of shops, typically once a day – a laborious process indeed.

A distinguishing feature of these machines is the capacity to modify the grind size by adjusting the distance between the upper and lower burrs. When the burrs are positioned closely, they yield a fine grind; when spaced farther apart, the output is coarser. Considering the diverse nature of coffee beans, there isn't a one-size-fits-all grinding approach. However, certain grinds are more compatible with specific coffee qualities. Additionally, the optimal grind size for a batch of coffee beans can be influenced by factors like its moisture content and age.

Flat and conical burr grinders are the primary options available in the market. The choice between the two largely hinges on the anticipated grinding volume within a specific time frame. Flat burr grinders are better suited for consistent grinding throughout the day. In contrast, conical burr grinders excel under high-demand scenarios, especially during peak times when the grinder operates almost continuously. Both designs can either come equipped with a doser or function "on demand," delivering 0.2 to 0.5 ounces (7–15 grams) of coffee directly into the coffee machine's filter as required. The latter design is gaining traction as it mitigates the oxidation of powdered coffee, which transpires when the ground coffee lingers in the doser. Additionally, these models simplify the cleaning process.

WAYS OF MAKING COFFEE

THE LONG JOURNEY TO ESPRESSO COFFEE

While our focus is narrowed to the two primary coffee species – Arabica and Canephora (often referred to as Robusta) – it's intriguing to think of coffee as a vast congregation of unique entities. Every bean is distinct due to its genetic makeup, intertwined with the specific climatic conditions, soil type, and even the sunlight exposure of each individual drupe. Compounding this complexity, coffee fruits can undergo numerous processing methods. Further, the beans' qualities can shift based on storage conditions and roasting levels. Finally, the chosen method of preparation significantly determines the sensory characteristics of the coffee we savor in our cups.

Over time, these variables have constantly evolved, influenced by shifts in climate, economic landscapes, societal changes, and the advent of innovative techniques and technologies.

Let's embark on a historical journey to trace coffee's evolution, endeavoring to envision the potential sensory profiles of the diverse brews enjoyed throughout the ages.

DRUPE DECOCTION

A decoction made from coffee drupes was likely the earliest method of crafting a coffee drink. This brew not only tapped into the healthful properties of the plant but also made water somewhat beneficial by infusing it with a rich blend of organic acids, minerals, and even carbohydrates.

However, such a coffee drupe decoction bears little resemblance to the coffee we're familiar with today. This is partly because it lacks the aromatic nuances introduced by roasting, and also because it leans more towards a bitter and astringent profile than a sweet one. It's possible that those early coffee drinkers only selected ripe drupes, which contain about 23-25% sugar. Nonetheless, this method was time-consuming and often resulted in a less than palatable beverage.

Today, coffee decoctions are still occasionally made, primarily using the husk of dried and lightly roasted drupes. Some individuals might have a taste for it, but it's a far cry from the robust coffee flavors we relish today.

A tinplate coffee pot with a wooden handle of the kind used in the eighteenth and nineteenth centuries. This kind of early and rudimental pot brewed coffee by infusing it in boiling water.

SEED DECOCTION

In the early 19th century, the Parisian magistrate and food aficionado, Brillat Savarin, stipulated that coffee should be brought to a boil three times. This traditional brewing technique, often referred to as Turkish coffee, has been honored by UNESCO, earning a spot on the world's intangible heritage list.

This approach certainly extracts the utmost from coffee, which, for this particular method, should ideally be ground to a somewhat coarse consistency to yield a clearer beverage.

However, this method is by no means quick. From a sensory perspective, it presents a couple of challenges. Firstly, there's the possibility of ingesting bits of coffee grounds while drinking. Moreover, some of the coffee's delicate aromas may dissipate during the boiling process, potentially allowing for a pronounced "overcooked" coffee scent to dominate.

In this Cezve-like copper pot, coffee was extracted by infusing it in boiling water.

This type of coffee pot known as Dellal was used for five centuries in all regions of Arabia, Syria and Mesopotamia.

PERCOLATED COFFEE

The aspiration of enjoying a cup of coffee without the unpleasant experience of coffee powder entering one's mouth prompted many to seek solutions. For instance, a French textbook from 1832 detailed the use of gelatin to clarify coffee – a method the author conceded resulted in the loss of much of coffee's finest aromas.

To address this challenge, the most straightforward solution was to pour hot water over coffee grounds placed in a filter chamber, which would contain them. This approach proved effective, and percolation has become today's most widespread coffee-making method, albeit executed with various tweaks and tools.

Naturally, the extraction of the coffee beverage is tied directly to the grind size of the beans. The finer the grind, the lengthier the brewing process. This entails brewing a large batch of coffee at once to ensure availability, leading to a diminished sensory experience. Coffee that's heated or maintained at a certain temperature for extended periods tends to lose much of its distinct flavor and attributes.

To circumvent this problem, nineteenth-century inventors diligently sought ways to expedite the percolation process. Numerous solutions emerged, with several earning patents. Let's delve into some of the primary innovations.

Compared to regular percolation coffee pots, this 1854 invention patented by Griffiths & Co. of Birmingham assured higher water pressure during the extraction process.

With this type of 1850–1860 coffee pot you could brew coffee with the vacuum, press, percolation or filter system.

This exquisite French coffee pot (1820-1830) worked with a filter system. This innovation was an important evolution in the history of coffee preparation, separating the beverage from the ground beans.

This 1950s French coffee pot brewed coffee by percolation. The chamber above the filter was removed after the coffee was brewed and the porcelain pot was sealed with its coordinate lid.

The base of this coffee pot is in aluminum, while the removable upper part could complement an elegant table spread. This 1960–1970 coffee machine extracted the beverage through steam pressure.

GRAVITY

The quintessential design of a classic coffee percolator resembles an inverted cone. Naturally, the coffee grounds situated within this cone will have varying thickness levels, resulting in differential resistance to the passage of water and thus leading to inconsistent coffee extraction.

As water navigates through the coffee grounds, it can cause shifts and clumping, creating channels as it's pulled downward by gravity. With these challenges in mind, inventors aimed to achieve a consistent layer of coffee grounds and uniform dispersion of the hot water that seeps through. Enter the advent of the first filter coffee maker, surprisingly attributed to the Archbishop of Paris, Jean-Baptiste de Belloy.

In 1802, Henrion took a different route, patenting a dual-chamber coffee maker designed to retain the coffee's warmth. This concept was subsequently discarded by Hadrot in 1806. Nonetheless, Hadrot refined the device's design, integrating a press mechanism capable of adjusting the density of the coffee layer, ensuring uniform water distribution. Addressing another sensory concern, Hadrot tackled the metallic aftertaste often imparted by the iron coffee pots of the era. This off-taste resulted from the iron reacting with the coffee's phenolic acids. To counter this, Hadrot introduced a coffee pot equipped with a filter made from a tin and bismuth alloy.

Early twentieth-century tinplate
Neapolitan flip coffee pot.

Early twentieth-century French flip nickel-plated brass coffee pot. Known as "Russian egg," this coffee pot came with a structure that allowed the rotation necessary to brew the beverage.

With Hadrot, the idea of crafting coffee machines with a metallic filter gained traction. A notable innovation came from the tinsmith Morize in 1819. He patented a unique coffee pot design that required inverting, merging the container used for heating water and the one for collecting coffee. This design can be seen as a precursor to the Neapolitan flip coffee pot.

While improvements to the panel and water distribution sped up the coffee-making process, the primary desire remained: to brew a robust cup of coffee without excessive use of grounds. Achieving this hinged on three primary factors: the temperature of the water, the fineness of the coffee grind, and the duration of interaction between the water (as the solvent) and the coffee grounds.

If you take boiling water off the heat and expose it to a cold surface (like the layer of coffee

WAYS OF MAKING COFFEE

This 1920-1930 German electric coffee machine brewed coffee through continuous pumping and percolation.

it needs to pass through), the water's temperature will drop. While this doesn't significantly impact the speed of brewing, it does affect the strength of the final beverage. Today, brewing at slightly lower temperatures is often seen as advantageous, but historically, the perspective was different. The flip coffee maker mitigated the issue of the water cooling down too much, but in 1819, Laurens introduced another solution. He invented and patented a coffee machine with a circulation pump that featured a sealed lower chamber. In this design, water was heated by a lamp and then forced into a manifold, from which it was distributed over the coffee in the upper chamber. Another innovation came in 1837 from Madame Jeanne Richard, who designed a coffee pot that could regulate the coffee's strength by recirculating it over the grounds. This method produced a notably robust brew, though it lacked some finesse in flavor.

VACUUM COFFEE POTS

In the first half of the 19th century, coffee brewing techniques began to harness the power of a vacuum in hermetically sealed two-chamber systems. One chamber held the water, which was positioned over a heat source, while the other chamber contained the coffee grounds. Once the water was sufficiently heated, the pot was removed from the heat. As the water cooled, it created a vacuum effect, drawing the water up into the second chamber with the coffee. Numerous patents for these vacuum coffee machines were registered, and they became particularly popular when they could be reliably made from durable glass. Occasionally, these models were constructed from metal, but that was more the exception than the norm. While this method expedited the brewing process, the coffee pots themselves were delicate and could be somewhat cumbersome to handle and clean, making the overall process a bit lengthy. That said, coffee brewed in these vacuum pots was often considered superior in terms of taste. Additionally, the brewing process was visually engaging, which might explain why this style of coffee pot remains popular in parts of Asia. Many modern cafes in the region feature updated versions of these pots that are more user-friendly.

This vacuum coffee machine was patented in 1855 in Vienna. Its "scales" structure made the entire coffee making process mechanical.

HYDRAULIC PRESSURE

The first hydraulic pressure coffee pots were developed in 1830 by the Frenchman, Count Réal, and later in 1854 by the Englishman, Loysel. Their designs brewed coffee by establishing a column of water situated above the coffee grounds. This innovative process had the notable advantage of allowing for a much finer grind, thereby enhancing the efficiency of the coffee extraction. Of the two inventors, Loysel's design gained significant popularity. Elegant and grandiose versions of his coffee pot were manufactured throughout the 19th century and beyond.

Late nineteenth-century British silver plate Napierian coffee maker.

VAPOR PRESSURE

The potential of steam has been recognized since the days of the ancient Greeks. However, the 19th century truly heralded the age of steam, marked by significant innovations like the steam engine, which efficiently replaced animal power in numerous domains. The realm of coffee-making was no exception, with inventors eagerly incorporating steam into the coffee brewing process – a procedure which typically demands both heat and water.

One of the earliest known patents for a steam-based coffee-making device was filed in 1932 by Louis Bernard Rabaud. He devised a coffee pot in which water was driven through the coffee grounds by vapor pressure, essentially paving the way for the future Italian moka pot. Follow-ing Rabaud's pioneering design, numerous inventions surfaced, includ-ing Samuel Parker's fountain coffee machine in 1833, Alexandre Lebrun's coffee pot in 1838, Giovanni Maria Loggia's creation in 1857, Eike's double-chamber coffee pot in 1878, and larger coffee machines, such as those devised by Angelo Moriondo in 1884 and Luigi Bezzera in 1905.

These advancements set the stage for the espresso coffee we're familiar with today. Although these machines typically operated at pressures just under two atmo-spheres, they delivered coffee more rapidly and ensured a supe-rior extraction process. However, their reliance on high temperatures posed a challenge, as such condi-tions can degrade the delicate aro-mas locked within plant cells.

MECHANICAL PRESSURE

Steam is an excellent resource, but not the optimal one for coffee. Francesco Illy realized this in 1935 when he patented a machine that used compressed air. In 1947, Achille Gaggia patented a coffee

Produced between 1920 and 1930 by La Lombarda, this electric coffee maker brewed coffee using steam pressure.

103 top This Italian 1960s electric coffee maker could simultaneously pour four coffees out of its spouts.

103 bottom This mid twentieth-century coffee maker with incorporated alarm was produced by Gaude, Turin: at a set time an electric resistance would activate, pouring the coffee into the cup, and in turn the cup with its weight would set off the alarm.

This Italian Belle Époque coffee machine could brew either two or four cups of coffee at a time.

This 1905 coffee machine, one of the first designed for bars, is characterized by its vertical shape and by the gas burner to create pressure in the chamber.

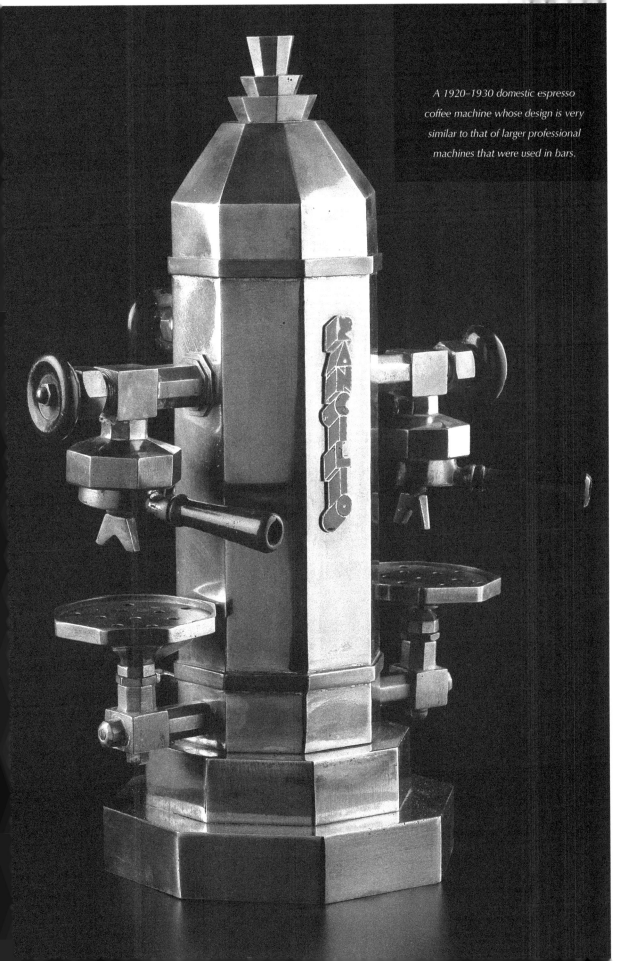

A 1920–1930 domestic espresso coffee machine whose design is very similar to that of larger professional machines that were used in bars.

machine with a spring mechanism capable of exerting a pressure of about eight atmospheres on the water.

This innovation, combined with the advancements achieved by hundreds of coffee roasters over the course of a century, eventually led to the birth of Italian Espresso coffee. The final step was taken by Faema in 1960, which invented a machine that applied pressure through a volumetric pump. The following year, the historic Faema E61 was introduced to the market.

PERCOLATION, INFUSION, DECOCTION:
WHAT ARE THE DIFFERENCES?

When discussing coffee, the following terms are often used interchangeably, but they shouldn't be. Each refers to distinct extraction techniques. Let's delve into each:

- percolation: This technique involves extracting flavors by allowing a fluid to pass through a porous substance.

This 1950s coffee machine worked by manual pressure. The water had to be heated separately and then pushed through the ground coffee by lowering the two levers.

WAYS OF MAKING COFFEE

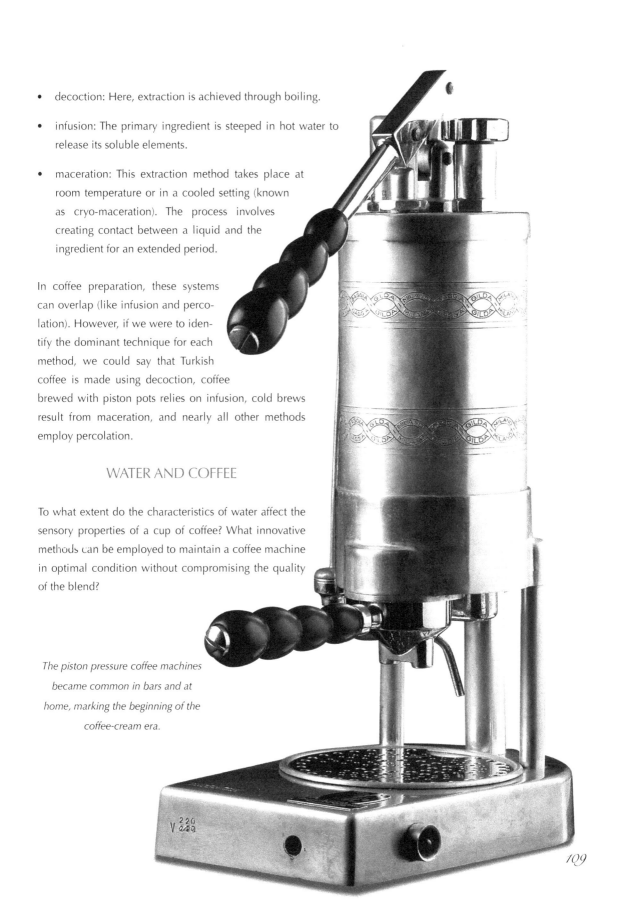

- decoction: Here, extraction is achieved through boiling.

- infusion: The primary ingredient is steeped in hot water to release its soluble elements.

- maceration: This extraction method takes place at room temperature or in a cooled setting (known as cryo-maceration). The process involves creating contact between a liquid and the ingredient for an extended period.

In coffee preparation, these systems can overlap (like infusion and percolation). However, if we were to identify the dominant technique for each method, we could say that Turkish coffee is made using decoction, coffee brewed with piston pots relies on infusion, cold brews result from maceration, and nearly all other methods employ percolation.

WATER AND COFFEE

To what extent do the characteristics of water affect the sensory properties of a cup of coffee? What innovative methods can be employed to maintain a coffee machine in optimal condition without compromising the quality of the blend?

The piston pressure coffee machines became common in bars and at home, marking the beginning of the coffee-cream era.

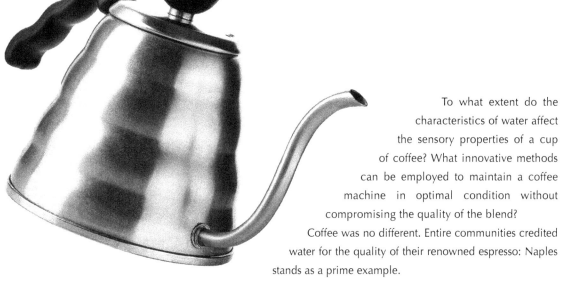

To what extent do the characteristics of water affect the sensory properties of a cup of coffee? What innovative methods can be employed to maintain a coffee machine in optimal condition without compromising the quality of the blend?

Coffee was no different. Entire communities credited water for the quality of their renowned espresso: Naples stands as a prime example.

Water, the quintessential solvent for coffee, undeniably plays a pivotal role. So, let's delve into the mechanisms governing the water-coffee relationship in espresso making.

THE CHARACTERISTICS OF WATER AND ITS INTERACTION WITH COFFEE

There are three primary aspects of water that influence the preparation of espresso coffee:

- presence of chlorine: Chlorinating water is a measure for public health, but it doesn't enhance the quality of our coffee cup. Even though the concentration of dissolved chlorine in drinking water has decreased over time, this element retains potent oxidizing power. The effect amplifies with heat, impacting the fats and affecting the formation of the crema.

- presence of anomalous smells: Unusual odors in water can result from various substances. Among the most disruptive are sulfur compounds, which directly compromise the sensory attributes of coffee, masking the floral and fresh fruity notes.

- presence of calcium and magnesium salts: These increase water hardness.

The adverse effect of chlorine is its tendency to reduce the crema in espresso coffee and mask a range of delightful aromas, especially the floral notes that many coffee enthusiasts cherish.

The issue of anomalous odors is more pronounced. Typically, their presence should indicate that a specific water source shouldn't be used. Sensory-wise, these odors can diminish aromatic intensity, obscure various aromatic nuances, or even introduce atypical scents that would otherwise remain undetected.

Two primary solutions exist for chlorine and anomalous odors: using water that's free of chlorine and odors, or employing pitchers and activated carbon filters designed to remove them.

Now, let's delve into the third factor: water hardness. It stems from a mix of anions (like sulfates and carbonates) and cations (such as calcium and magnesium). These elements split into two categories: permanent and temporary hardness. Together, they define the overall hardness of the water, a metric typically found in standard test kits.

Permanent hardness primarily comes from calcium sulfate, which remains even when the water is heated. In contrast, temporary hardness arises from carbonates, which can lead to deposits or scale forming on coffee machine components when heated.

This brings us to a crucial dilemma: while hard water can produce superior coffee, it can be detrimental to the upkeep and efficiency of espresso machines. Calcium plays an essential role in achieving a full-bodied coffee with a rich, stable, and elastic crema. This cation aids in forming a protein matrix that, when coffee is poured, captures carbohydrate colloids. Due to the action of the remaining carbon dioxide in the coffee and the difference in weight density, this matrix rises, forming the crema.

The usual method to soften water involves substituting calcium with sodium. This cation behaves differently, especially when the pH drops, resulting in increased acidity. Sodium can be particularly harsh on metals and tends to produce a watery coffee with a thin, inelastic crema. To strike a balance between making exceptional espresso and maintaining machine health, innovative solutions have been developed for both professional and home settings: filters that simultaneously guard against scale and eliminate undesired substances.

COFFEE MAKING METHODS

As we've observed, coffee has always been a beloved beverage. Over the centuries, humans have strived to perfect the brewing process, innovating various methods based on their understanding, available resources, and cultural beliefs. This journey has led to a myriad of techniques, each unique in its approach to this natural product, and each producing distinct outcomes. Apart from the decoction of the drupes, there isn't a singular, dominant method for making coffee. Different cultures embrace different techniques.

ESPRESSO COFFEE

A cup of espresso coffee is made by forcing water through a layer of coffee, producing a multi-layered beverage filled with soluble, suspended, and emulsified compounds. While all coffee types exhibit these characteristics, espresso coffee accentuates the suspended and emulsified compounds. Additionally, it is distinguished by the unique relationship it forms between these and the soluble compounds.

By the late nineteenth century, coffee had been a staple in Western countries for at least three centuries. Over this span, numerous brewing methods had been conceived. However, perfecting the brew was no simple task. The objective wasn't just about creating a coffee infusion. The process needed to be swift, ensuring the coffee was enjoyed fresh while preserving all its flavorful extractions, and leaving the least desirable components in the spent grounds.

In essence, the coffee industry labored for roughly three centuries to fulfill three deeply interrelated needs:

- Rapidity: While it's true that coffee is especially appreciated for its caffeine, the quickest way to obtain it from the plant would be to eat a coffee leaf salad or a few cherries, whether raw or boiled, as was customary in earlier times. With today's globalization, we could certainly arrange for fresh deliveries of these items daily. However, only the most adventurous palates might appreciate such offerings. The true game-changer was the idea of roasting the seeds. Through roasting, coffee beans acquire the distinctive aroma we all recognize and love. What's more, only minimal amounts of water are needed to extract coffee's finer elements. Hot or cold water? Both work, but cold water takes longer. While cold extraction has been known since 1832, it's a slower technique and thus less commonly used. Conversely, it's evident that using hot water speeds up brewing. By increasing pressure, water can exceed its boiling point, which accelerates the extraction process and intensifies the brew. However, this method, though faster, can produce a coffee that's more bitter and astringent, resulting in the loss of some delicate aromas.

- Strength: Human senses rarely misjudge the physiological effects of food, and coffee is no exception. Historically, a robust coffee has always been associated with a pronounced effect on the nervous system. The potency of coffee is gauged by three aspects: aroma intensity, consistency (often referred to as body or syrupiness), and bitterness. Three variables can influence the potency of a coffee cup: the species (Canephora beans – to which Robusta belongs – yield a more robust coffee than Arabica), roasting, and extraction. Darkly roasted Robusta beans produce a more potent cup, but one that might feel less pleasant to the palate.

It's known that in the early stages of coffee's presence in Europe (around the 1600s), Arabica was the sole option. However, it seems it might not have been the best one. A French nobleman, while a guest of the Ambassador of Sultan Mehmed, found the coffee so unsavory that he felt compelled to sweeten it with a bit of sugar from a nearby bowl. This simple act transformed the flavor so dramatically that, from 1669 onwards, even the Ambassador adopted the practice.

Sugar doesn't just counteract bitterness mentally; it also enriches the body and prolongs the aroma's persistence. This was so widely recognized that, as noted by German anatomist and botanist Johann Vesling in 1638 during a visit to Cairo, sugar was already in use in Egypt, where they even candied coffee cherries. However, coffee was a luxury product, and its users aimed to maximize its yield. This wasn't primarily achieved through roasting, which, given the means available then, was likely a rough process with many over-roasted beans. Instead, they optimized through extraction: the coffee was boiled repeatedly, sometimes up to ten or twelve times. Initially, coffee was prepared the Turkish way: water was boiled in the iconic double truncated-cone copper pot, then mixed with coffee grounds. The mixture was then re-heated until boiling, cooled, and heated again. Brillat Savarin advised against repeating this process more than thrice. However, while Savarin was indeed a connoisseur, he was also wealthy. The less affluent repeated the boiling process multiple times, if only to savor the coffee's aroma.

- Pleasure: When something resonates well with us, our brain marks it as beneficial, leading us to enjoy it even if there are counteracting signals that would typically reduce our pleasure level. This explains our acceptance of bitterness in beer, certain liqueurs, and coffee. However, when bitterness pairs with astringency (that unwelcome dry sensation in the mouth), the product becomes less palatable. Historically, the choice of coffee species wasn't as crucial as it is today with the prevalence of Robusta. Yet, inconsistent roasting, which often resulted in burnt beans, combined with repeated boiling of the coffee-water mixture, undoubtedly compromised the brew's enjoyment. While the coffee grounds' presence in the beverage intensified its strength, it also made the drink less pleas-

WAYS OF MAKING COFFEE

ant upon sipping, enhancing its bitterness and astringency. Over time, enhancements were made to coffee pot designs to optimize brewing, with filters added to the spouts to refine the beverage's quality. However, this didn't entirely address the issue. The ideal coffee was envisioned as black, piping hot, freshly brewed, and not reheated. There was also the challenge of the coffee's fatty components turning rancid. This degradation can occur in beans mere days after roasting (unless protected), in ground coffee just hours post-grinding, and in the brewed drink within minutes.

ESPRESSO FROM THE BAR

Certainly, the rise of espresso coffee and its global popularity wasn't solely due to the desire for quick coffee. A perfectly prepared cup of espresso remains an unparalleled delight. While the filter system holds its dominant position globally, it's estimated that over two million professional espresso machines exist today. By "professional machines," we refer to those under the care of a barista responsible for selecting and grinding the blend, skillfully operating the machine. We're not referencing the super-automatic electronic espresso machines, which, though efficient and advanced, lack the human touch that so enriches the espresso experience.

However, the evolution of coffee machines has undoubtedly influenced the development of espresso coffee. To this day, a superior coffee machine can distinguish the quality of the brew.

The espresso machine, central to the espresso method, boasts Italian origins. Giovanni Loggia showcased a steam coffee machine at the 1857 Brescia exhibition. In 1884, Angelo Moriondo patented a large-scale coffee machine tailored to the demands of a bustling café. In 1901, Milanese engineer Luigi Bezzera further refined this machine, patenting his enhanced version. By 1970, the coffee world saw the advent of multi-boiler machines. The purpose of this technological advancement was to achieve peak stability paired with thermal adaptability, thus elevating the resulting brew. In these devices, the generation of steam was distinct from the water heating process for brewing. The 1980s witnessed the debut of the first super-automatic machines, some equipped with integrated doser grinders.

Nowadays, technology continually shapes the evolution of coffee machines, ushering in heightened automation and precise temperature control. This allows baristas to tailor the end product to exact specifications. Presently, the market offers various systems to heat water for espresso, including the heat exchanger system, the lever system, and the separate boiler system.

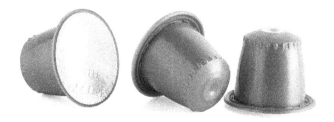

CERTIFIED ITALIAN ESPRESSO

A traditional Italian Espresso is characterized by a dark brown hue crowned with a tawny, hazel-colored cream. This cream is remarkably fine, boasting a dense texture devoid of bubbles. The aroma is captivating, emitting distinct notes of flowers, fruits, toasted bread, and chocolate. These aromatic impressions linger, persisting for several seconds or even minutes after the sip. In terms of taste, it is well-rounded, full-bodied, and velvety. The acidity and bitterness harmoniously balance each other, ensuring neither overshadows the other, and any astringency is minimal or entirely absent.

This description is endorsed by the Italian National Espresso Institute, established in 1998, to encapsulate the epitome of espresso coffee and guarantee consumers an unparalleled experience. The Institute also offers a comprehensive chart spanning blends, doser grinders, machines, and barista standards.

Bar-served espresso coffee isn't a pre-made beverage; it's crafted on the spot. Therefore, the role of the barista is paramount in delivering an impeccable coffee experience. The barista is entrusted with selecting the blend, calibrating the doser grinder for the perfect grind consistency, and setting the machine's temperature and pressure. Furthermore, a barista's senses, combined with a few critical physical parameters, are integral to the process. To achieve the quintessential espresso, a barista should produce 0.5 fl oz (25 ml) of coffee within 25 seconds, utilizing water heated to approximately 194 °F (90 °C) and exerting a pressure of 9 bars.

ESPRESSO AT HOME

The espresso we brew at home today is a direct descendant of the coffee served at our favorite cafes, though it often doesn't achieve the same level of perfection. The explanation is straightforward: for economic reasons, household appliances must be more affordable and user-friendly, which can result in slightly compromised performance. Presently, there are two primary methods for making espresso at home: using capsules and operating automatic machines.

CAPSULES

At the end of the 20th century, making espresso at home became simpler with the introduction of coffee pods – single servings of ground coffee compressed within a paper filter. This innovation made preparing espresso quick, easy, and closely comparable to what you might find at a cafe. Moreover, it set the stage for the proliferation of single-origin coffees, allowing enthusiasts to sample distinct flavors and deepen their understanding of beans from various regions. The subsequent development was the advent of espresso capsules: 0.1 to 0.2 oz (5–7 g) of coffee encased in small, uniquely shaped plastic or metal containers. These are designed to be placed into specialized machines that dispense pressurized water for roughly 15 seconds.

Today, pods and capsules constitute a significant portion of the global coffee market. They're even gaining traction in cafes, especially in places where, due to high demand or other factors, a professional espresso machine might not be the best fit.

AUTOMATIC ESPRESSO MACHINES

These innovative machines can quickly grind 0.1 to 0.3 oz (5–10 g) of coffee and brew a cup of espresso in just 15 to 20 seconds. Compared to coffee capsules, this approach has a reduced environmental footprint, and over time, after recouping the initial investment, it can result in notable savings. Additionally, it offers consumers the opportunity to delve into single-origin coffees and discover new tastes.

OTHER TYPES OF ESPRESSO

Espresso coffee has become a global phenomenon with millions of espresso machines in use. However, not all espresso is like the Italian version. In Italy, you'd use 0.2 oz (7 g) of coffee powder to brew 0.5 fl oz (25 ml) of coffee. Yet, in other countries, a standard espresso might use 0.3 oz (10 g) of coffee powder or even more. In some cultures, an ideal espresso can measure up to 1.6 fl oz (50 ml) in the cup.

Additionally, technically speaking, even the coffee dispensed by vending machines (like those found in workplaces and many public areas) qualifies as espresso. Sadly, in many instances, compromised commercial priorities have led to a significant drop in espresso coffee quality. This subpar experience often results from the low-quality coffee used in these machines and their improper cleaning and maintenance. Modern machines come equipped with advanced extraction technology, which, if used right, could yield an excellent cup of coffee.

THE FILTER SYSTEM

The filter system involves brewing coffee through the gravity percolation of water, which is typically preheated to around 203°F (95°C). This method uses approximately 0.3 to 0.5 oz (10–15 g) of coffee to produce a roughly 6.7 fl oz (200 ml) cup. It's an ideal choice for those who enjoy a larger volume of coffee: the brew is light-bodied, but when done right, offers minimal bitterness, well-balanced acidity, and a satisfying aroma. This brewing style is prevalent globally, particularly in regions with high coffee consumption like Northern Europe and the United States.

Historically, the filter method emerged as the third primary coffee brewing technique. While boiling the fruit of the coffee plant, or drupes, didn't yield a sensory-pleasing result and was mainly favored by those

in coffee-growing regions, boiling ground roasted coffee beans often led to a drink with gritty remnants. To address this, in the 1700s, people began placing coffee inside a cloth bag which was then submerged in boiling water. A man named Donmartin enhanced this approach by attaching the bag to the top of a coffee pot, typically positioned above a small burner to maintain warmth.

Coffee held such significance that even the archbishop of Paris, Jean Baptiste Belloy (1709–1808), felt compelled to design his own coffee pot. He introduced a straightforward yet highly effective innovation: the pot was divided into two chambers. The bottom chamber was cylindrical, featuring a spout equipped with a stopper and handle. The upper chamber, also cylindrical, housed a filter at its base and was capped with a lid. This design allowed for brewing a coffee rich in aroma. Due to its success, Belloy's coffee machine quickly became the gold standard for coffee makers, and variations of it remain in use today. The design was later refined by Henrion and Hadrot in the early 19th century.

The filter system, rooted in gravity percolation, paved the way for numerous subsequent systems, each boasting its own advantages and drawbacks. Examples include the coffee powder placed in a canvas cone filter into which boiling water was poured, the double-chamber coffee maker that suspended the coffee via a metal filter, and the double filter system designed to achieve a more consistent layer of coffee. There was also the immersion filter, ideal for brewing large quantities, though it typically offered a higher yield at the expense of quality. Concurrently, innovators were developing new water heating methods. These inventions eventually gave rise to electric machines capable of dispensing hot water over the coffee and the introduction of novel filter types.

Today, the simplicity of this brewing method has broadened the horizons significantly. From the single-dose kits popular in Japan (and in other parts of the world) that come with a cup, filter, coffee, sugar, and powdered milk – ready to be used wherever there's access to hot water – to large coffee machines designed to brew vast amounts of coffee for community gatherings and conferences.

In the realm of coffee aficionados and the diverse methods of coffee preparation and serving, we've witnessed the rise of filter systems that rely on both skill and finesse. Some of these are also somewhat theatrical, adding an element of showmanship, and have been embraced by cafes as a means to introduce newcomers to unique coffee experiences. Let's delve into the primary filter systems, both traditional and contemporary.

NEAPOLITAN FLIP COFFEE POT

History relies on written records, and the invention of the Neapolitan flip coffee pot is traced back to 1819, credited to a Frenchman named Morize. However, it's uncertain whether this technique existed beforehand or if it was popular in Naples. Regardless, this style of coffee pot became iconic in Naples. This might be attributed to the city's preference for strong roasts, which yield a coffee rich in aroma even when brewed using a filter coffee maker. Conversely, the penchant for robust-flavored coffee might have prompted Neapolitans to roast their beans longer to harness the full flavor potential of the flip coffee pot. While it relies mainly on gravity and is slower, it lacks the extraction power of a moka or espresso machine. Originally, Neapolitan flip coffee pots were crafted from copper, but by 1886, aluminum became the material of choice. Today, stainless steel variants dominate the market.

Commonly referred to as the *cuccumella*, this coffee pot typically boasts a cylindrical design, comprising one chamber for water, another for the brewed coffee, and a central section for the coffee grounds, which uses a double filter system to facilitate the flow of water through the coffee.

To brew coffee with a Neapolitan flip coffee pot, begin by filling the water chamber. This chamber has a small hole, which not only prevents internal pressure buildup but also indicates when the water has boiled. Next, add coarsely ground coffee to the filter, seal it, and place it in its designated section. After attaching the collection chamber for the brewed coffee, the pot is ready for heating. Once the water boils, flip the coffee pot to let gravity pull the hot water through the coffee grounds, allowing the brewed coffee to collect in the now-lower chamber. This brewing process can take anywhere from 5 to 10 minutes, primarily influenced by the coarseness of the coffee grounds.

CHEMEX

A direct descendant of the Erlenmeyer flask used in chemistry, the Chemex coffeemaker was invented in 1941 in Germany by Dr. Peter Schlumbohm. The Chemex is a single glass receptacle in the shape of two truncated cones: a larger one at the bottom, where the brewed coffee is collected, and a smaller, open one on top, where the filter is positioned.

Chemex coffeemakers are available in various sizes, serving from three to six cups of coffee. The ideal ratio calls for 0.5 oz (15 g) of coffee per cup. Here's how to make four 6.7 fl oz (200 ml) cups of coffee: start with one liter of hot (203 °F/95 °C) water and place the paper filter in the upper cone of the pot. Rinse the filter thoroughly with some of the hot water, allowing it to pass through the paper, and then discard that water.

Add the coffee to the filter and pour some of the hot water over it in a spiraling motion until the coffee grounds are fully saturated. Wait for 45 seconds, then pour another quarter of the water and wait once more. You can also gently stir the wet grounds with a wooden spoon, but remember to wait for 30

seconds after each water addition before pouring more. Once you have 28 fl oz (800 ml) of brewed coffee in the lower cone, your beverage is ready to be served.

It's worth noting that Chemex paper filters are thicker compared to those used in other filter methods. This thickness slows down the brewing process, contributing to greater extraction. Additionally, Chemex coffeepots can also be used with metal filters, which need to be washed and thoroughly dried after each use.

V60

The V60 coffeemaker is named after its V-shaped top section with a 60° angle, designed to hold the filter. Below this section is where the brewed coffee is collected.

Start by heating 21 fl oz (300 ml) of water to 203 °F (95 °C). Place the paper filter in the top section and rinse it with about 3.5 fl oz (100 ml) of the hot water to remove any paper taste. Discard this water. Add roughly 0.4 oz (13 g) of coarsely ground coffee. In a controlled circular motion, pour about 0.8 fl oz (25 ml) of the hot water over the coffee grounds and let it sit for 30 seconds. Repeat this pour, wait another 15 seconds, and continue until you have 7 fl oz (200 ml) of brewed coffee collected below. If the grind is right, the entire process should take between 2.5 and 3 minutes. A longer brew time indicates too fine a grind, while a shorter time suggests the grind is too coarse.

INFUSION, DECOCTION AND MACERATION

Coffee enthusiasts have endlessly experimented with the beloved beverage, leveraging a myriad of classical techniques developed over centuries to extract the best and healthiest elements from this natural product. While some of these methods have gained immense popularity, others remain niche favorites. However, the passion for experimentation within the coffee community shows no signs of waning. As we anticipate future innovations, let's delve into the primary preparation methods stemming from the aforementioned techniques.

FRENCH PRESS

The French press, commonly known as a piston coffee pot, features a glass container housed in a metal frame. This frame stands on four legs, raising the vessel off the surface. The pot is equipped with a piston that incorporates a filter bordered by a spring. This spring's primary function is to prevent coffee grounds from bypassing the filter and mixing into the brewed coffee.

The process is simple: begin by preheating the glass container with some hot water. Then, add 0.4 oz (14 g) of coffee to the glass. Pour in 7 fl oz (200 ml) of water heated to 203 °f (95 °c), ensuring that the coffee grounds are uniformly saturated. Let it steep for 4 minutes. After steeping, skim off any foam that forms on the surface. Attach the piston and press it down, compacting the coffee grounds at the bottom of the pot. Your coffee is now ready to be poured. The final brew's body and aroma will vary based on the coarseness of the coffee and the steeping duration. Additionally, the clarity of the coffee will depend on both the expertise of the person making it and the quality of the french press used.

CLEVER COFFEE DRIPPER

This brewing method, originating from Taiwan, involves a glass cone that sits atop a vessel or mug to collect the brewed coffee.

Start by heating water to a temperature between 194–198 °F (90–92 °C). After placing the paper filter inside the cone, use some of the heated water to rinse the filter thoroughly. Add 0.4 oz (14 g) of ground coffee to the cone, then pour 7 fl oz (200 ml) of the hot water over the grounds. Allow the coffee to steep for two and a half minutes before letting it filter through. The entire process should take approximately one minute.

AEROPRESS

This brewing technique is one of the more recent coffee-infusion methods. Invented in 2005 by Alan Adler, it features a cylinder that concludes with a filter and an internal piston.

The brewing process is straightforward: First, heat water to a range of 194–200 °F (90–93 °C). Use some of this hot water to rinse the filter before attaching it to the cylinder. Add 0.4 oz (14 g) of appropriately

WAYS OF MAKING COFFEE

ground coffee to the cylinder, then pour in 7 fl oz (200 ml) of water, ensuring the coffee grounds are uniformly saturated. Allow the coffee to steep for 1 minute. Afterward, press the coffee through the filter using the piston, dispensing the brewed coffee directly into a cup. One of the perks of this method is its adaptability, letting you fine-tune the sensory profile of the coffee to your preference.

SYPHON

Originating in the first half of the 19th century, the siphon coffee-making method is undeniably one of the most visually impressive. A siphon coffee maker consists of two chambers – typically two spherical glass vessels – stacked vertically and connected by a central filter.

To brew coffee using this method, start by adding 10.5 fl oz (300 ml) of water to the lower chamber. On top, in the upper chamber, add 0.5 oz (15 g) of ground coffee. Next, light a flame beneath the lower chamber to boil the water. As the water heats, pressure will force it upward into the upper chamber, saturating the coffee grounds. Once all the water has transitioned to the upper chamber, extinguish the heat. The cooling process will create a vacuum in the lower chamber, pulling the brewed coffee from the upper chamber through the filter and back down below. Once this process is complete, your coffee is ready to be served.

For a quicker brew time (roughly 90 seconds), consider starting with pre-heated water.

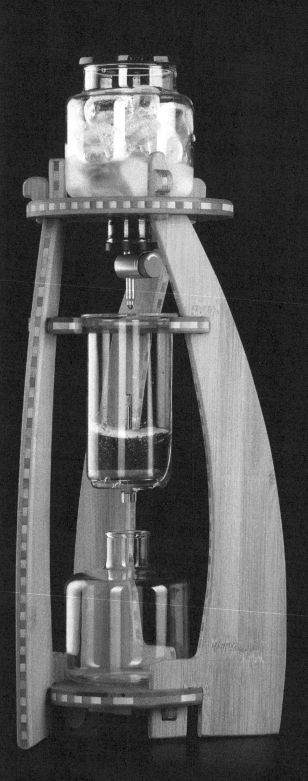

COLD BREW

A 1832 manual describes the cold-extraction coffee technique, highlighting how this method completely altered the sensory properties of the beverage by reducing the levels of bitter and astringent components, while greatly preserving the aroma. The reason this method didn't gain traction is its lengthy process: to make one quart of coffee, it can take anywhere from 6 to 24 hours, depending on individual taste preferences. This method has seen various adaptations and numerous recipes have been introduced on the occasion of its bicentennial.

The cold brew equipment, sometimes referred to as cold drip (though purists point out there are distinctions between the two), primarily consists of a water chamber (which can be filled with just water, water and ice, or only ice) positioned above a filter holding coffee grounds. Directly below is a container to collect the brewed coffee. The initial step involves filling the filter with relatively coarse coffee grounds and thoroughly wetting them with water. Subsequently, position the collecting vessel below and adjust the tap to release the brewed coffee at a rate of 6–10 drops every 10 seconds (roughly 0.1 fl oz/3 ml per minute). The ideal coffee-to-water ratio is approximately 2.4 to 3.1 oz (70–90 g) per 35 fl oz/1 liter, which translates to 0.2 to 0.3 oz (7–9 g) per 3.5 fl oz/100 ml.

WAYS OF MAKING COFFEE

GOTA A GOTA

This method hails from Peru and utilizes a cylindrical coffee maker made up of two almost equally-sized chambers. Coffee is filled in the top chamber. Then, with practiced skill, boiling water is added gradually and repeatedly until the bottom chamber is brimming with essence. In this technique, the brew truly resembles a coffee essence, a syrup that can retain its quality for up to 72 hours. This concentrated essence can then be diluted with hot water according to one's preference. The process demands patience as the hot water needs to be added in regular intervals, specifically when the coffee grounds begin to dry out. Additionally, only minimal amounts of water are added each time, ensuring that just a small amount of liquid emerges from the coffee grounds.

The outcome is a sensorially intriguing brew, but it's imperative that the coffee grounds are of top-notch quality, properly roasted, and finely ground.

TURKISH COFFEE

This method is the second oldest in coffee making, right after brewing directly from the coffee fruit. Technically, Turkish coffee is a decoction since it's made by boiling coffee grounds in water. While UNESCO designated it as "Turkish coffee" in their list of intangible heritage, this technique is practiced in many parts of the world, each with its unique twist, rooted in centuries of tradition. It's prevalent in many Middle Eastern countries, throughout the Balkan peninsula, and, naturally, in Turkey.

To make Turkish coffee, you use a distinctive copper or brass long-handled pot called an "ibrik" or "cezve." Traditionally, it's heated in hot sand, but most people today use other heat sources. Pour 1.7 fl oz (50 ml) of water per cup into the pot and bring it to a boil. Then, add a teaspoon of coffee and let it return to a boil. Once you remove the cezve from the heat, the boiling subsides, allowing you to skim off the foam that forms on top. Boil it once more, and then it's ready to be served. Before drinking, wait a few minutes to let the grounds settle at the bottom of the cup.

MOKA POT

The moka system operates on a steam-pressure principle. Specifically, steam generated by boiling water in the pot's lower chamber forces the water through a layer of coffee grounds. The moka pot owes its design lineage to the innovative contributions of several inventors, including Louis Bernard Rabaud of France, Romershausen from Germany, England's Samuel Parker, France's Lebrun, Italy's Angelo Loggia, and Eike of Germany. The modern version of the moka pot, as we recognize it today, was brought to life by Bialetti in 1933.

Before Bialetti's patent, Italians primarily brewed their coffee using percolation machines, with the Neapolitan flip coffee pot as the most popular choice. However, the moka, initially and mistakenly referred to as "the Milanese" coffee pot, quickly gained prominence. We'll delve into the notable differences between the two shortly, but first, a clarification is in order: the moka coffee pot originated in Piedmont, specifically in Omegna, a town celebrated for its skilled metalworkers. With the Neapolitan flip coffee pot, gravity simply pulls the hot water through the coffee grounds into the lower chamber. This method isn't just slow – even a minor error in the coffee grind, or changes to the coffee due to humidity, can significantly prolong the brewing time. And when you're craving coffee, every second counts. Furthermore, once the pot is removed from the heat and flipped, the boiling water in the top chamber starts to cool, reducing its extraction efficiency.

In the moka pot, the opposite occurs: as the water heats, pressure builds due to its struggle to pass through the coffee layer. This results in a superior extraction, producing coffee with a richer aroma and fuller body.

Compact, affordable, and efficient enough to match the speed of today's world, the moka pot effectively draws out the best qualities from coffee beans. It's no wonder then that the moka pot has seen immense success, difficult as that might be to quantify. Consider this: roughly 15 million moka pots are sold globally each year.

If we assume the average lifespan of a moka pot is around ten years, that suggests there could be as many as 150 million working moka pots worldwide, or about one for every ten households. However, since not everyone globally partakes in moka coffee, the actual percentage would likely be significantly higher, especially when factoring in cultures with a strong preference for this drink. For instance, in Italy, 90% of households reportedly own moka pots, and many have multiple sizes.

Of the annual 15 million moka pots manufactured, Italy accounts for the sale of 10 million, firmly establishing its dominance in this sector with approximately 25 producers and 30 active brand names. Elsewhere, around 15 producers can be found in countries such as Spain (home to about five producers), Latin America, Germany, and a handful of other nations.

THE MOKA POT: COMPONENTS AND TECHNIQUE

Essentially, the moka pot consists of a bottom chamber where water is heated, a central funnel-shaped filter filled with coffee grounds, and an upper jug-shaped chamber where the brewed coffee is collected. This top section has a central collector through which the coffee rises.

The underlying principle of the moka pot is the transition of water from liquid to steam. Without heat, the air and liquid inside the lower chamber below the filter are in balance. However, as the temperature increases, pressure builds. The water's only escape is through the base of the funnel-shaped coffee filter. Once the internal pressure is sufficient to counteract atmospheric pressure and the resistance posed by the layer of coffee grounds, the liquid rises into the upper chamber where the coffee is collected.

Once all the water has moved to the upper chamber, steam follows, releasing the signature puff that signals it's time to turn off the heat.

A quality moka pot should meet the following criteria:

- Maximum water temperature during extraction: 209°F (98°C).

- Maximum pressure within the lower chamber: 2.5 bar.

- Maximum temperature of the brewed coffee: 185°F (85°C).

- Maximum volume of coffee brewed per dose of coffee grounds: 1.6 fl oz (50 ml).

- Amount of water remaining in the bottom chamber after extraction: approximately 0.1 fl oz (5 ml) per cup.

HOW TO CHOOSE THE PERFECT MOKA POT

Stainless steel or aluminum? On the surface, this appears to be the primary decision when selecting a moka pot. However, there are numerous other vital factors to evaluate, many of which influence the sensory qualities of the brewed coffee and the longevity of the coffee pot itself.

Let's delve into these considerations:

- material: While stainless steel may appear more aesthetically pleasing, simpler to clean, and more durable compared to aluminum, sensory tests have frequently favored aluminum. It's essential to note that aluminum quality varies, so it's critical to factor this in. Beyond the base material, there are other nuances to account for:

- finterior finish (particularly in the lower chamber): A smoother finish is preferable because it's easier to maintain and clean. Irregularities such as rough spots, scratches, indentations, and other imperfections can impact the pot's lifespan and, over time, the sensory profile of the coffee.

- gasket: The gasket is virtually the only component of a moka pot that experiences wear, especially if you secure the coffee pot with coffee grains on the edge of the filter. When the gasket deteriorates, the pot no longer maintains an airtight seal. During the brewing process, it becomes challenging to achieve the necessary pressure for the coffee to ascend, leading to excessive steam release and a minimal amount of coffee in the collection chamber. Although replacing the gasket might seem simple, it can be tricky with a severely worn-out rubber. Nowadays, besides rubber gaskets, there are also Teflon ones available. They offer a significantly improved seal and are notably heat-resistant – an advantage for those moments the moka pot is inadvertently left on the burner. Generally, they also last longer.
- handle: The design and position of the handle are crucial to prevent potential burns and ensure a firm grip. Another vital consideration is how the handle is attached to the pot. Being the component most vulnerable to damage from either an intense flame or extended exposure to heat, its attachment method is significant. If the handle is secured with screws, it's easy to replace. Otherwise, once damaged, repairs become quite challenging.

MOKA POT: DIFFERENT SHAPES AND PERFORMANCE

The moka method is definitely a brilliant one and its success has led manufacturers to produce countless versions of it to meet different needs: there are moka pots that make half a cup of coffee and there are models that can brew up to 18.

The moka method is undoubtedly ingenious, and its widespread success has prompted manufacturers to introduce a myriad of versions to cater to various preferences. Moka pots range from those that produce just half a cup of coffee to models capable of brewing up to 18 cups. There are even oversized demonstration moka pots that can churn out 50 cups. Given the intricacy of this coffee maker (as discussed in a specific section), scaling its size, whether making it miniature or gigantic, isn't always a straightforward task. This implies that even if one maintains a consistent volume and design ratio, the outcome might differ. Typically, the three-cup moka pot yields the best performance. However, through meticulous studies on the process's kinetics, some manufacturers have managed to calibrate both the smaller and larger models, thereby minimizing variations in performance. In fact, the differences become so slight they're almost indistinguishable in scientific sensory analysis tests.

Typically, the filter holds 0.1 oz (5 g) of coffee powder per cup. However, it's possible to use up to 0.4 oz (13 g) of ground coffee for one or two cups, resulting in a more pronounced sensory experience.

HOW TO USE A MOKA POT AT ITS BEST

When posed with the question about the most challenging dish to perfect, a renowned chef reportedly responded, "fried eggs." While the authenticity of this tale remains uncertain, one truth emerges: simplicity often demands the greatest attention to detail.

Making a cup of coffee with a moka pot may seem like one of the simplest tasks in the kitchen, but brewing an exceptional cup requires expertise. Where should one begin? The immediate answer might be to start with high-quality coffee grounds. After all, if the coffee isn't top-notch and specifically suited for the moka pot, no amount of effort will yield the desired result. We'll delve deeper into this in the next section.

Assuming you have a quality moka pot, a reliable heat source, fresh coffee, and water, what's the next step? First, thoroughly rinse each part of the moka pot: the funnel filter, the upper filter (where the gasket is located), the collection chamber, and the base. Then, fill the base with water, either up to the valve or to a designated marker (some moka pots feature one). If you adhere to this guideline – and if your moka pot is well-designed – you'll need roughly 1.6 fl oz (50 ml) of water for each cup of coffee.

Now, position the filter atop the lower chamber. Here's where things can get a bit tricky: adding the coffee. If the coffee is in a soft packet, the optimal approach is to pour it directly into the filter, forming a mound that rises above the filter's edge. Gently tap the pot so that the mound settles evenly with the filter's rim. It's essential to remove any excess coffee grounds from the edge of the filter and the base. Any leftover grounds can impart a burnt flavor to the brewed coffee due to the heat. Additionally, these stray grounds might reduce the chamber's pressure, affecting the brew's quality and potentially damaging the gasket. Finally, attach the top section to seal the moka pot.

If you're sourcing the coffee powder from a jar, you'll want to use a spoon that fits well. In some situations, it might be necessary to press down on the coffee within the filter. It's essential to aim for an even layer of coffee, without any spots being denser or thinner than others. Uneven distribution could cause the water to flow more freely in certain areas, leading to over-extraction in some parts and under-extraction in others. This inconsistency could adversely affect the taste of your coffee. That's why the often-mentioned trick of making three holes with a toothpick is neither useful nor productive.

Once you've properly filled the filter with coffee, attach the upper section and set the moka pot on your heat source. But what kind of heat should you use? The key is ensuring the heat source is moka pot-friendly. If using a gas stove, ensure the flame doesn't exceed the pot's base. This precaution prevents the handle from scorching, and more importantly, it provides a consistent and gentle warmth to the water, allowing it to permeate through the coffee

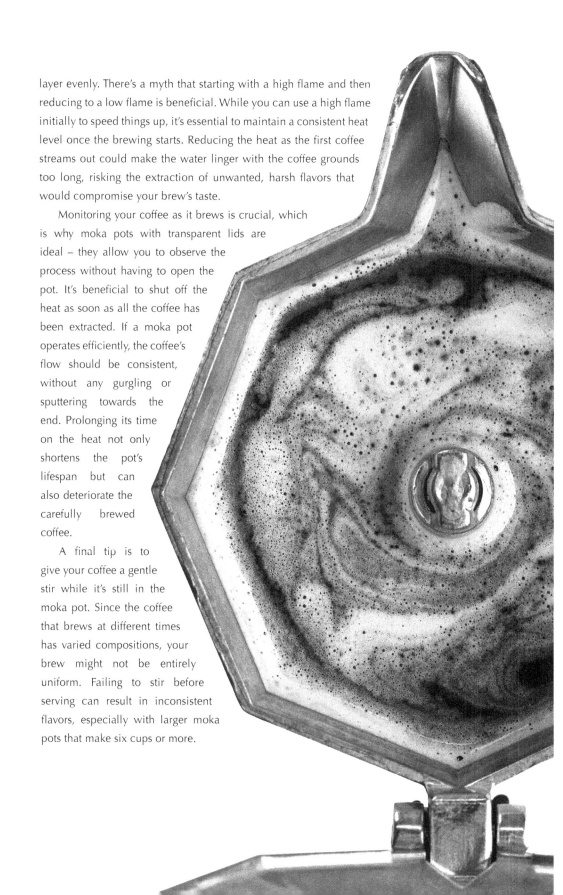

layer evenly. There's a myth that starting with a high flame and then reducing to a low flame is beneficial. While you can use a high flame initially to speed things up, it's essential to maintain a consistent heat level once the brewing starts. Reducing the heat as the first coffee streams out could make the water linger with the coffee grounds too long, risking the extraction of unwanted, harsh flavors that would compromise your brew's taste.

Monitoring your coffee as it brews is crucial, which is why moka pots with transparent lids are ideal – they allow you to observe the process without having to open the pot. It's beneficial to shut off the heat as soon as all the coffee has been extracted. If a moka pot operates efficiently, the coffee's flow should be consistent, without any gurgling or sputtering towards the end. Prolonging its time on the heat not only shortens the pot's lifespan but can also deteriorate the carefully brewed coffee.

A final tip is to give your coffee a gentle stir while it's still in the moka pot. Since the coffee that brews at different times has varied compositions, your brew might not be entirely uniform. Failing to stir before serving can result in inconsistent flavors, especially with larger moka pots that make six cups or more.

COFFEE AND THE SENSES: HOW TO ENJOY A GOOD CUP OF COFFEE

COFFEE TASTING: AN ART ACCESSIBLE TO ALL

For those deeply passionate about coffee, whether due to professional commitments or sheer love for the beverage, a single hot cup can convey a wealth of information. It can reveal the specific Coffea species that gave rise to the beans, perhaps even hint at the origin of the beans. It can tell tales of the methods and machinery involved in producing the green coffee, the discerning selection and expertise in roasting, and even the prowess of the person who brewed that particular cup. Every one of these variables manifests in the intricate interplay of thousands of molecules present in the coffee, giving rise to unique combinations – or distinct sensory cues – that we can identify using a mental map each of us can cultivate.

Coffee tasting, then, is an art open to anyone keen on mastering it. It welcomes those humble enough to recognize the endless scope for learning, and those willing to be mentored by individuals for whom coffee is more than just a beverage – it's a calling. Our goal here, however, is somewhat more modest. We aim to offer insights that enable both professionals and enthusiasts to sketch the sensory characteristics of an Italian-style coffee cup, gauge its hedonic qualities, and adeptly interpret the nuances it presents to our senses. In this endeavor, we'll be guided by the principles established by the International Institute of Coffee Tasters, established in 1993, which has since educated eleven thousand students across more than forty countries.

COFFEE CUPPING

The method of coffee cupping, or tasting, carries significant weight, given the impressive sensitivity of our sensory organs and the cognitive capabilities of our brain. Adjusting the procedure can shift both the intensity and the nature of our sensory experiences. For instance, holding a coffee cup closer to our nostrils as compared to another modifies the blend of molecules that our olfactory system detects and interprets. Similarly, the volume of a coffee sip can influence our perception of its body and other characteristics.

While we don't aim to drastically change the practices of coffee tasters, it's vital to recognize certain standards and adhere to them during evaluations. Here's a step-by-step guide to a proper cupping procedure:

- STEP 1 - Observing the Coffee: Once the coffee is served, resist the urge to move the cup. Instead, observe the color and the texture of the cream, if present. Reflect on the visual appeal of the beverage.

- STEP 2 - Aromatics: Gently lift the cup to your nose and take a deep sniff for roughly 3 seconds. Gauge the aroma's intensity and its pleasantness.

- STEP 3 - First Sip: Slurp approximately 0.1 fl oz (5 ml) of the coffee, allowing it to spread across your palate before swallowing. Assess the coffee's body, acidity, and bitterness.

- STEP 4 - Second Sip and Aftertaste: Slurp another 0.1 fl oz (5 ml) and let it move around your mouth. As you swallow, keep your mouth slightly ajar. Reflect on the aftertaste and, circling back to the mouthfeel, evaluate its astringency.

- STEP 5 - Overall Evaluation: Contemplate the coffee you've tasted. How pleasurable was the experience?

THE ECOSYSTEM FOR COFFEE TASTING

When it comes to sensory analysis, nothing is more perfect than a human. As of today, no instrument or piece of equipment has managed to rival the capabilities of a person. Regrettably, the human being, complex in its biology, possesses diagnostic capacity and sensitivity that aren't always complemented by a brain adept at memorizing and recalling past sensations. Moreover, the human brain is continuously processing thoughts and is influenced by emotions, even when engaged in a professional sensory evaluation. Such thoughts and emotions can undeniably sway judgment.

Therefore, it's crucial to conduct tastings when one is well-rested, calm, and relaxed. The environment plays a significant role as well: it should be lit adequately, ideally with natural sunlight or a light source of similar quality. The absence of overpowering or unusual odors is essential, as they can interfere with the evaluation process.

Regarding the timing of the tasting, it's worth noting that while coffee is often enjoyed after a hearty meal, when it comes to analysis, it should be tasted between meals. Nonetheless, the taster shouldn't be so hungry that their judgment becomes clouded.

CUP OR ESPRESSO CUP?

The size of the cup, naturally, hinges on the amount of coffee being tasted. However, the shape and size are crucial in capturing all the nuances coffee presents. Let's delve into the factors that contributed to the design of the taster's cup for Italian Espresso.

Espresso should be presented in an espresso cup. While some restaurants might attempt to differenti-ate their service with larger cups, it's technically more accurate to serve this revitalizing drink in cups ranging from 2.5 to 3.3 fl oz (75–100 ml), given that an average serving should be around 0.8 fl oz (25 ml). This cup size is also fitting for tasters assessing a sample, as long as the cup adheres to the recommended capacity, its design follows the right geometry (a smaller diameter preserves the cream and directs the aroma to the nose), and it's crafted from appropriate materials. Indeed, the cup plays a pivotal role: it influences the visual appeal of the cream, has an olfactory impact as it can either concentrate or disperse the aromas emanating from the drink, affects taste perception through the sensation determined by lip contact (notably regarding heat perception), and finally dictates how the beverage flows into the mouth. Numerous studies aiming to define the ideal coffee cup have been conducted. These studies have given us a clear idea of the ideal cup's characteristics. We've already discussed the cup's capacity. When it comes to materials, porcelain stands out as the best choice due to its durability (unlike earthenware cups, it doesn't chip easily), excellent thermal insulation, and the satisfying sensation it provides upon lip contact. The optimal geometry would be based on an elliptical section that tapers slightly at the top – at least internally, while maintaining an exterior bell shape to ensure smooth pouring into the mouth.

TASTING SPOON

In certain coffee cupping methodologies, particularly those associated with the Brazilian approach, the toolkit often features the goûte caffè or the tasting spoon, among other instruments. This spoon is occasionally asymmetrical, of medium size, broad and shallow, with a relatively elongated handle. However, the International Institute of Coffee Tasters chooses not to employ this spoon. Their rationale is that it fails to provide a comprehensive sensory evaluation of the beverage. Moreover, it poses some practical challenges (some tasters are averse to tasting from a shared cup) and could distort the true attributes of the coffee, making it misaligned with the consumer's perception.

COFFEE TEMPERATURE

The sensory evaluation of a cup of coffee should be conducted when it reaches a temperature of around 149°F (65°C). For espresso, considering that its temperature is about 176°F (80°C) once poured into the cup, two conditions are essential for accurate tasting: the sensory examination must start within roughly one minute of brewing, and the cup should be warm, but not scalding. As the coffee cools, the crema quickly dissipates, leading to a noticeable reduction in aroma intensity. This is accompanied by a significant shift in the olfactory profile and alterations in the tactile and taste balance. Tasting the same coffee at varying temperatures can yield different evaluations.

THE ART OF PERCEPTION AND ITS TOOLS

The environment generates stimuli that our sensory system captures through our sense organs, each specifically designed to detect a distinct type of physical or chemical energy.

When an external agent (distal stimulus) interacts with a receptor, it is converted into an electrical stimulus (proximal stimulus) via transduction. This transformed energy then travels to the brain, which decodes and structures it through fundamental cognitive processes and dynamic psychological mechanisms. This process results in perception. From this perception, behavior is formulated, leading to a reaction to the initial stimulus.

SENSORIAL EXPLORATION

The joy derived from sipping coffee is significantly amplified if we can identify each sensation and tie those sensations back to the coffee's origin, the methods utilized in processing the green beans, the roasting process, and the brewing of the drink itself. Where should one start? From sensory exploration. When we drink coffee, our brain often creates a singular perception that is typically expressed in a binary fashion (like/dislike, good/bad). However, a trained taster can dissect this perception for detailed analysis.

Embarking on this journey, which is open for everyone aiming to be a coffee taster, there are several tools developed over recent decades that prove invaluable. The most recent of these tools is the coffee tasting map.

Picture this: you have a cup of coffee before you and wish to capture every nuance. With the sensory map, the act of tasting transforms into an enthralling adventure, be it in the comfort of your home or at your favorite coffee joint. Using the map, you delve deep into the very essence of the coffee, reaching distant lands, and thereby heightening your coffee-drinking pleasure.

Furthermore, coffee tasting maps play a pivotal role in the promotion of the coffee industry – be it within companies, at trade shows, or other events. Coffee originating from a specific region or from a particular company can be detailed through a sensory map. This map can then aid in tastings, serve as an informative or aesthetic feature where the coffee is consumed or sold, and, of course, help illustrate the unique properties of the coffee to potential customers during tastings.

SENSORY EVALUATION: THE TASTING CARD

The tasting card serves as a compass, guiding tasters through their sensory evaluation journey while simultaneously providing a standard for gauging the product's unique characteristics. In the realm of food and beverages, a myriad of tasting cards exists – whether descriptive, parametric, structured-scaled, or otherwise. The scope and structure of a card can be tailored based on the purpose of the tasting or the expertise of the person creating it.

Currently, a multitude of coffee tasting cards are available, each varying in depth and focus, contingent upon the entities that develop them. Here, we'll delve into the newly crafted tasting card by the International Institute of Coffee Tasters: the "Trialcard plus." This tool proves invaluable for those embarking on the coffee discovery voyage.

Not only does this tasting card encompass the quintessential list of descriptors that gauge overall enjoyment (like allure, harmony of flavors, tactile balance, and refinement), but it also incorporates objective parameters that tie back to distinct elements of the coffee. These can be effortlessly mapped to factors like its origin, roasting style, and brewing method. By employing this card, one can pinpoint the individuality of each coffee and ascribe a hedonic value aligned with personal preferences. Moreover, the card empowers tasters by offering them the liberty to introduce new descriptors, thereby personalizing and enriching their tasting experience.

SENSORY EVALUATION

For a taster, and indeed for a discerning consumer, understanding the relationship between sensory perception and the production process is crucial. This understanding not only enhances enjoyment and appreciation but also deepens retention. Greater knowledge invariably leads to an enriched memory of the experience. Thus, we'll begin by delving into the intricacies of the sense organs, understanding sensory perceptions, and exploring their connections with the nuances of raw materials and production methodologies.

SIGHT AND VISUAL EVALUATION

Sight is a physical sense that allows perception of the external environment using a form of electromagnetic energy known as light.

The primary organ responsible for interpreting these signals is the eye, which facilitates our sense of sight.

Light passes through the cornea and the crystalline lens before reaching the retina, which houses two primary types of sensitive cells:

- cone cells: These are sensitive to color and detail, primarily serving our daytime vision.
- rod cells: These provide a less detailed vision and require less light, making them primarily responsible for vision in low-light conditions.

SENSORY MAP OF ESPRESSO COFFEE

ISTITUTO INTERNAZIONALE
ASSAGGIATORI CAFFÈ

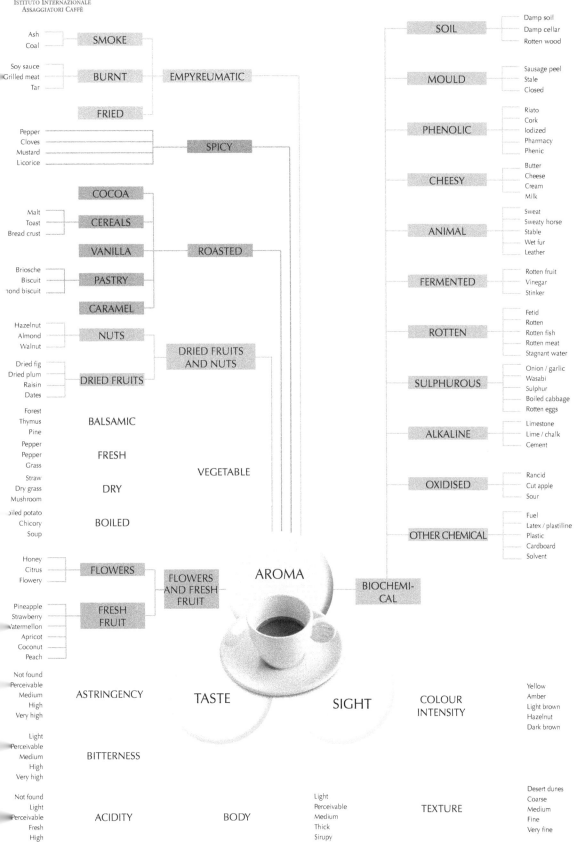

SMOKE
- Ash
- Coal

BURNT — EMPYREUMATIC
- Soy sauce
- Grilled meat
- Tar

FRIED

SPICY
- Pepper
- Cloves
- Mustard
- Licorice

COCOA

CEREALS
- Malt
- Toast
- Bread crust

VANILLA — ROASTED

PASTRY
- Briosche
- Biscuit
- Almond biscuit

CARAMEL

NUTS
- Hazelnut
- Almond
- Walnut

DRIED FRUITS AND NUTS

DRIED FRUITS
- Dried fig
- Dried plum
- Raisin
- Dates

BALSAMIC
- Forest
- Thymus
- Pine

FRESH
- Pepper
- Pepper
- Grass

DRY
- Straw
- Dry grass
- Mushroom

BOILED
- Boiled potato
- Chicory
- Soup

VEGETABLE

FLOWERS
- Honey
- Citrus
- Flowery

FLOWERS AND FRESH FRUIT

FRESH FRUIT
- Pineapple
- Strawberry
- Watermellon
- Apricot
- Coconut
- Peach

AROMA

BIOCHEMI-CAL

SOIL
- Damp soil
- Damp cellar
- Rotten wood

MOULD
- Sausage peel
- Stale
- Closed

PHENOLIC
- Riato
- Cork
- Iodized
- Pharmacy
- Phenic

CHEESY
- Butter
- Cheese
- Cream
- Milk

ANIMAL
- Sweat
- Sweaty horse
- Stable
- Wet fur
- Leather

FERMENTED
- Rotten fruit
- Vinegar
- Stinker

ROTTEN
- Fetid
- Rotten
- Rotten fish
- Rotten meat
- Stagnant water

SULPHUROUS
- Onion / garlic
- Wasabi
- Sulphur
- Boiled cabbage
- Rotten eggs

ALKALINE
- Limestone
- Lime / chalk
- Cement

OXIDISED
- Rancid
- Cut apple
- Sour

OTHER CHEMICAL
- Fuel
- Latex / plastiline
- Plastic
- Cardboard
- Solvent

ASTRINGENCY
- Not found
- Perceivable
- Medium
- High
- Very high

TASTE

SIGHT

COLOUR INTENSITY
- Yellow
- Amber
- Light brown
- Hazelnut
- Dark brown

BITTERNESS
- Light
- Perceivable
- Medium
- High
- Very high

ACIDITY
- Not found
- Light
- Perceivable
- Fresh
- High

BODY

SIGHT
- Light
- Perceivable
- Medium
- Thick
- Sirupy

TEXTURE
- Desert dunes
- Coarse
- Medium
- Fine
- Very fine

COLOR INTENSITY OF THE CREAM

The color saturation level of coffee cream ranges from pale yellow, which is considered zero, to monk's tunic brown, which represents the maximum saturation level.

Color saturation is more pronounced in dark-roasted Robusta. For Arabica, the saturation is more intense with perfectly matured coffee that is rich in sugars and proteins and contains a moderate amount of monochloric acids. Naturally, the roasting level is also a decisive factor for Arabica.

TEXTURE OF THE CREAM

When visualizing the coffee's cream as a piece of fabric, the texture can be likened to the density of the weave. Irrespective of the quantity and consistency, a denser weave signifies a greater texture. The pinnacle of texture is achieved when the weave is indistinguishable because the cream resembles colored whipped cream. This parameter is particularly relevant for coffees that feature a cream topping, which is a hallmark of quality in Italian Espresso.

Arabica coffee typically boasts a very fine texture. This is especially true when the coffee is mature, rich in fats, and contains an ample amount of sugars and proteins. The roasting process also plays a role: slow and thorough roasting brings out the finest texture in the beans.

PERSONAL PREFERENCE

This attribute is hedonic in nature, essentially dictating how enticing the coffee appears at first glance.

For seasoned tasters and industry professionals, personal preference might diminish if the color is either too intense or too muted, and if the texture appears sparse. Such visual cues can suggest the use of dark or lightly roasted Robusta in excessive amounts, the incorporation of immature beans, hasty preparation, and other potential missteps.

SENSE OF SMELL AND OLFACTORY EVALUATION

The sense of smell operates as a chemical sensory system, founded on receptors situated on an approximately 0.7 square inch (2 square centimeters) mucous membrane at the base of the nose. Olfactory molecules access the olfactory epithelium in three distinct manners: orthnasal, retronasal, and via blood supply. The orthnasal path is direct, commencing with the dual nostrils and nasal cavities which subsequently divide into three posterior nasal apertures. Within these cavities, air undergoes filtration, moistening, and turbulence, thanks to the posterior nasal apertures. The retronasal approach originates in the pharynx and converges with the orthnasal path, thereby producing a distinct draft. The blood supply method is facilitated by vessels that hydrate the olfactory epithelium with blood.

Upon the engagement of an olfactory molecule with the olfactory villus, the chemical energy metamorphoses into an electrical signal that reaches the brain via the olfactory bulb.

The potency of the olfactory sense is truly remarkable:

- It predominantly overshadows other senses.

- It boasts an almost boundless spectrum, being receptive to more than 400,000 molecules.

- Its sensitivity surpasses even that of instruments used in chemical research, with a detection threshold of 1 ppt (1 part in 1,000,000,000,000 parts).

- Its response time is notably swift, clocking in at 400 milliseconds.

- It remains alert even during slumber.

- It directly affects the brain's right hemisphere and the limbic system, which house our memory and emotions.

- It also operates on a subliminal level, meaning non-perceptible molecules can still impact our behavior and physiology.

Among the general floral notes, the citrusy floral components are often predominant.

However, the sense of smell has attributes that make it challenging for tasters to harness, like its rapid adaptability, its inverse correlation semantics, its emotional undertones, and its cultural biases.

The olfactory dynamics concerning coffee are intricate. Instruments have pinpointed over a thousand molecules, and as technology advances, more are continually being unearthed. The influence of these chemical entities is contingent on their concentration, their interrelation, and the sensitivity of the individual taster. This implies that a singular molecule often doesn't result in a unique aroma; in numerous instances, it can evoke a range of different scents.

OLFACTORY INTENSITY

The total olfactory volume refers to the collective intensity of aromas, regardless of their specific nature or characteristics. This volume is influenced by every raw material and procedure that contributes to the generation of potent aromatic compounds.

Flowers and Fresh Fruit

Floral and citrus notes, as well as hints of honey and either general or specific fresh fruit aromas, are predominantly associated with washed, medium to dark roasted Arabica coffee. These particular notes fade with intense roasting and are not adequately expressed during light roasting.

Vegetable

Fresh vegetable aromas (like pea, capsicum, and freshly cut grass), dried vegetable scents (such as straw, hay, and mushroom), boiled vegetable hints (like potato and chicory), and balsamic vegetable nuances (reminiscent of forest and aromatic herbs) are most pronounced in unripe Robusta and Arabica coffees. These vegetable notes can be particularly strong in coffees with certain defects. However, some specific coffee origins exhibit distinctive and, often, desirable vegetable tones.

Nuts and Dried Fruit

The perception of nuts, such as walnuts, almonds, and hazelnuts, as well as dried fruits like dates, figs, and prunes, is predominantly found in washed Arabica coffee. It can also occasionally be detected in naturally slow-roasted Arabica coffee.

Vegetable notes may include peas, peppers, grass, leaves, boiled potatoes…

Roasted

Perception of cereals, including malt, toasted bread, and bread crusts, as well as caramel, vanilla, cocoa, and pastries like croissants and biscuits, is linked to the degree of coffee roasting. Natural roast levels tend to produce cocoa and cereal notes. Overly dark roasting can diminish certain notes and introduce empyreumatic (burnt) characteristics.

Spice Notes

Perception of general spices, or specific ones like pepper, cloves, mustard, and licorice, is somewhat tied to the coffee's species and origin. Additionally, the presence of certain molecules related to these notes is influenced by the roasting process. As the roast becomes darker, these molecules shift their aromatic profile, transitioning from dried fruit notes to roasted ones.

Empyreumatic

Perception of fried (like fried oil) and burnt notes (such as grilled meat, ash, coal, smoke, and burnt rubber) primarily stem from the roasting method. Even a light roast, if not done properly, can impart empyreumatic aromas. Some coffee varieties, especially Robusta, are more prone to exhibiting flavors within the empyreumatic spectrum.

Other Biochemical Notes

A large category of defects that coffee might have includes the following notes: earthy, mildew, phenolic, caseous, animal, fermented, putrid, sulfurous, basic, hydrocarbon, oxide, and others.

Defects can develop at any stage, but they usually originate from a poor selection of green beans, whose defects are then amplified by roasting.

Spicy notes include licorice, pepper, cloves and cinnamon.

Global Positive Notes

The overall intensity of smells that come from high-quality raw materials and a skillfully executed production process.

Global Negative Notes

The overall intensity of smells that arise from compromised raw materials and an improperly executed production process.

Aroma Persistence

Aroma persistence refers to the length of time aromas remain detectable after the beverage has been consumed. This evaluation focuses solely on the lingering scents, excluding any taste or tactile sensations. Optimal aroma persistence is often found in mature coffees that have been roasted perfectly and possess a high lipid content. Interestingly, even coffees with defects can exhibit pronounced aroma persistence.

Finesse

This descriptor, based on hedonism, is inherently subjective and gauges the degree of refinement and pleasure derived from the aroma. The pinnacle of elegance and enjoyment in aroma is typically found in coffee that is perfectly matured, free from defects, and expertly roasted.

Richness

This descriptor is hedonic in nature, making it inherently subjective. It measures the complexity of the aroma by identifying the number of positive notes discernible in the coffee being evaluated. Richness is more pronounced in washed coffees, particularly those derived from beans that are mature, defect-free, and expertly roasted.

Hedonic Level

This descriptor is subjective and assesses the overall appeal of the coffee being evaluated. It correlates with the quality of the raw material and the accuracy of the production process.

POSTCENTRAL GYRUS SYSTEM AND TACTILE EVALUATION

The postcentral gyrus is a region of the brain responsible for receiving sensory input related to tactile sensations. The specific sensitivities it governs include:

- Tactile sensitivity

- Thermal sensitivity (heat and cold)

- Pain sensitivity

- Deep sensitivity (via proprioceptors, which detect the body's position in space)

- Visceral hypersensitivity (related to internal organs)

Tactile sensitivity offers a dual perspective: it provides physical sensations such as volume, viscosity, and texture, while also conveying chemical sensations. Common chemical sensations are classified as astringent (like the sensation from an unripe persimmon), pungent (like vinegar), spicy (as in chili pepper), metallic (similar to the sensation of a spoon on the tongue), and pseudo-thermal sensations (cold sensations as from mint, or warming sensations like those from alcohol).

Body

The body of coffee, often referred to as its viscosity, measures the thickness or fullness of the beverage on the palate. For reference, filtered coffee exhibits minimal body, while a high-extraction espresso boasts a maximum body. A coffee with a pronounced body typically stems from beans that are well-matured, abundant in fats, and rich in sugars and proteins, especially when they have been fully roasted. Conversely, underripe beans can contribute to a body that feels "off" or "negative" in quality.

Astringency

Astringency is a tactile sensation often felt within 15 seconds of sipping a beverage. It can manifest in various ways, including a change in saliva lubrication, a puckering or wrinkling sensation on the inner surfaces of the mouth, or a feeling of dryness known as xerostomia. This particular sensation is commonly associated with Robusta coffee and beans that are not fully matured.

Tactile Balance

Tactile balance refers to the well-rounded perception of the coffee in the mouth. Ideal tactile balance is achieved when no abrasive sensations, like astringency, are detected, and the mouthfeel is characterized solely by smoothness and silkiness. Coffees that have been expertly roasted, have lower levels of chlorogenic acids, and are abundant in fats and sugars tend to offer a superior tactile balance.

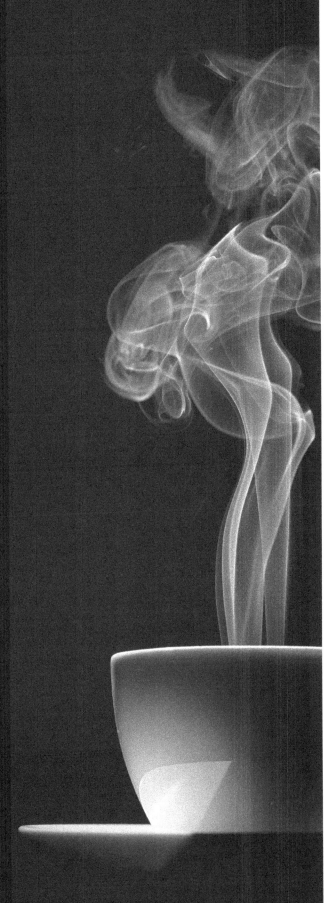

SENSE OF TASTE AND EVALUATION OF FLAVORS

The sense of taste is primarily situated within the mouth, specifically designed to detect molecules dispersed in liquids.

The majority of taste receptors, or papillae, are located on the tongue. Each papilla houses one or more taste buds, which in turn contain taste cells. These cells have microvilli that are sensitive to tasteful substances. When such a substance interacts with a microvillus, it initiates an electrical signal. This signal travels through the gustatory nerve and eventually reaches the brain where it is processed.

Taste parameters in coffee may seem straightforward, but they are crucial for coffee characterization. This is largely because they're more intuitive to discern compared to olfactory notes. Following visual assessments, taste is typically the next most accessible attribute to evaluate in coffee.

Acidity

A taste sensation likened to a brief, low-voltage electrical current across the tongue, which quickly fades, leaving behind a fresh aftertaste.

Acidity is more pronounced in coffee brewed from immature beans, those that have been washed or pulped (descascado), and beans that have undergone a light roast.

Bitter

A bitter sensation detected by the taste papillae.

This bitterness is more prominent in Robusta coffee, beans that are immature or flawed, and those that have been dark roasted.

Flavor Balance

This is a subjective, hedonic element that assesses the balance between acidity and bitterness. It hinges on the careful selection of coffee, the right blend of natural and washed coffees, and balanced roasting.

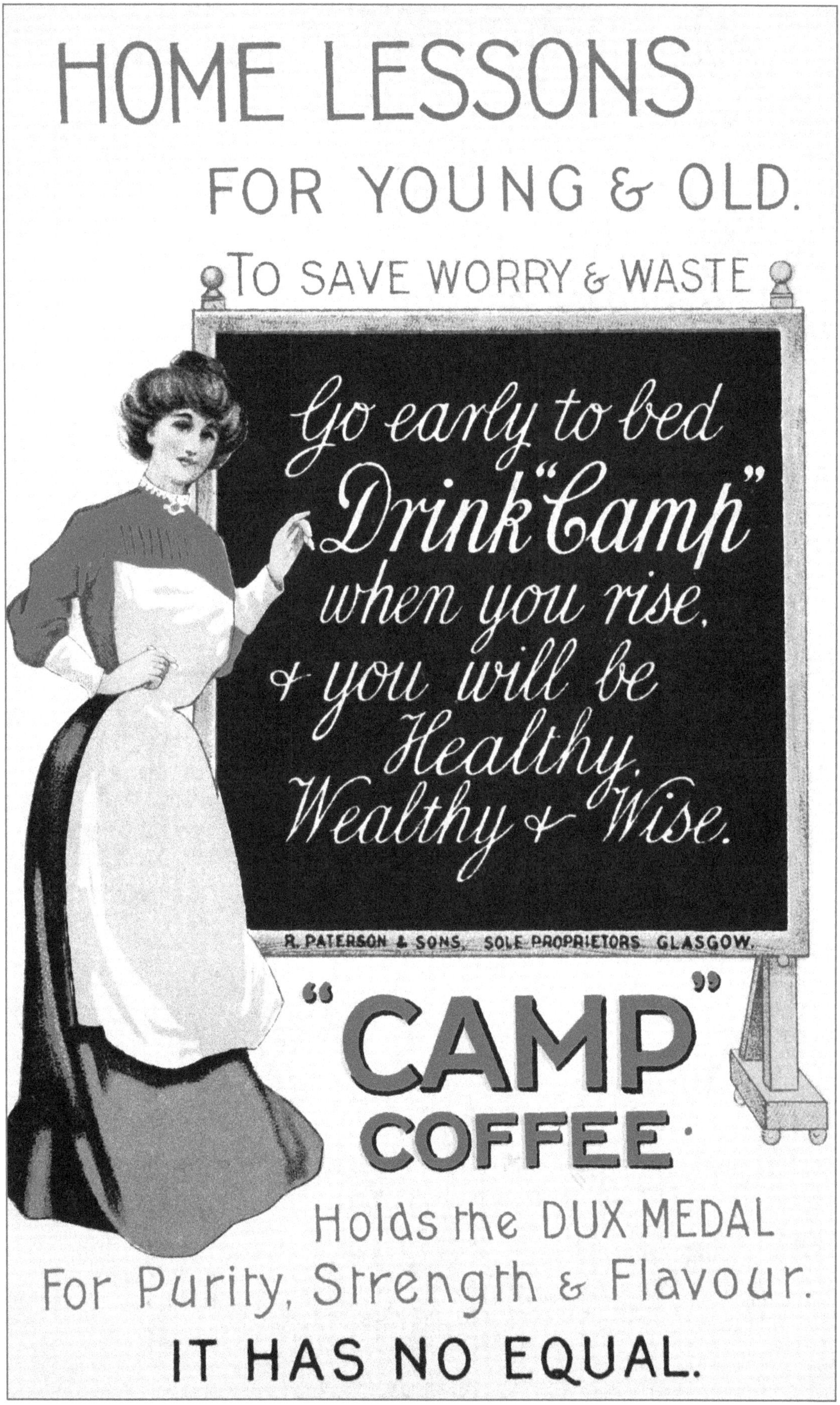
HOME LESSONS
FOR YOUNG & OLD.
TO SAVE WORRY & WASTE
Go early to bed
"Drink "Camp"
when you rise,
& you will be
Healthy,
Wealthy & Wise.
R. PATERSON & SONS. SOLE PROPRIETORS. GLASGOW.
"CAMP"
COFFEE.
Holds the DUX MEDAL
For Purity, Strength & Flavour.
IT HAS NO EQUAL.

COFFEE AND MILK

A PERFECT COMBINATION

Coffee has inspired countless brewing and preparation methods. We've touched on many of them, but several methods also involve pairing coffee with other ingredients. Among these, milk stands out as the most popular. In many countries, the combination of milk and coffee is nearly ubiquitous, accounting for 95% of total coffee consumption.

CAPPUCCINO

Cappuccino stands as the global champion among coffee and milk drinks. Crafting the perfect cappuccino begins with the right ingredients and equipment, but it's equally crucial to master the hands-on techniques involved. In seemingly straightforward preparations like this, any misstep can significantly impact the end result. While mastering the art of the perfect cappuccino may be challenging, it's undeniably a rewarding endeavor.

INGREDIENTS

COFFEE, OR RATHER, CERTIFIED ITALIAN ESPRESSO
While it's often said that a splash of quality milk can salvage a subpar coffee, the flip side is that the flaws of a coffee can be amplified in a cappuccino. This is due to the fact that compared to an espresso, a cappuccino contains a higher fat content. These fats bond with the aromatic molecules of the coffee, which, when released in the mouth due to salivation and tongue movement, activate olfactory senses. Our sense of smell, often operating subconsciously, deters us from consuming off-putting foods, even if we can't pinpoint why.

A substandard coffee blend might introduce undesirable compounds, like chlorogenic acid, which can disrupt the structure of frothed milk. This separation of milk components can then compromise the cappuccino's texture.

The foremost consideration is the choice of coffee blend. It should offer a robust aromatic presence, rich in desirable aromas, with an impeccable sensory

profile. Blends with off-putting aromas or those that are overly roasted and astringent should be sidestepped.

Another pivotal aspect is the preparation of the espresso, as well as the quantity used. It's imperative to adhere to the standard: 0.8 fl oz (25 ml) brewed over 25 seconds. A perfect cappuccino can't be crafted using a "lungo" (an extended brew that uses more water than a standard espresso).

In summary, the cornerstone of an exceptional cappuccino is a Certified Italian Espresso.

MILK

For a superior cappuccino, it's essential to use fresh, full-fat, premium-quality milk. The importance of milk goes beyond its volumetric contribution to the beverage; it fundamentally influences the sensory experience. With a fat content hovering around 3.5%, these fats not only bind and enhance aromas in both the milk and coffee but also, based on their globular structure, profoundly affect tactile sensations. These fats amplify the inherent creaminess and the much-adored velvety texture that lingers satisfyingly after consumption.

Proteins, present at about 3.2%, with their intricate branched structures, enable the milk to froth, playing a primary role in achieving that desired creamy consistency. Naturally, the aromatic compounds in milk meld seamlessly with those in coffee, fostering nuanced aromatic profiles and heightened levels of palatability. However, prolonged heating can transform not just the physical attributes but also the chemical makeup of the milk. For instance, prolonged heating can lead to an increase in molecules associated with smoky or burnt odors. While these might be imperceptible when the milk stands alone, they can become evident in a cappuccino due to their interaction with existing coffee molecules.

COFFEE AND MILK

To maintain its quality, milk should be stored chilled between 38–41 °F (3–5 °C) and be frothed straight from this cold state. When frothed correctly, 3.3 fl oz (100 ml) of milk should warm up to the optimal serving temperature of approximately 131 °F (55 °C) and expand to a volume of 4.2 fl oz (125 ml). Properly frothed milk for cappuccino boasts a density of roughly 0.6. Using previously heated milk for frothing can pose challenges: the resulting foam may lack creaminess, components might separate, and there's a heightened risk of over-heating the cappuccino.

SECONDARY INGREDIENTS

Cocoa, powdered chocolate, and other ingredients: are they truly essential? While we don't wish to stifle anyone's creativity, we firmly believe that incorporating various elements aside from espresso coffee (thus encompassing any alternative coffee preparation) and frothed milk results in distinct beverages, yielding more or less successful renditions of the traditional cappuccino.

EQUIPMENT

DOSER GRINDER AND ESPRESSO MACHINE

A doser grinder and an espresso machine are essential for crafting espresso coffee. However, an espresso machine must also provide the energy required for frothing milk. Frothing is achieved using a steam wand, typically equipped with 3, 4, or 5 nozzles at the end. Naturally, the machine's boiler must maintain the correct temperature to ensure the supply of an adequate quantity of steam with the appropriate thermal energy. Equally important is the length of the steam wand: if it's too short, it may not penetrate the milk frothing pitcher correctly, making the necessary frothing movements challenging to execute. Flexibility is crucial for the same reasons.

As for the nozzles, some experts recommend using wands with four 0.05-inch (1.5 mm) diameter holes to ensure sufficient pressure and prevent rapid temperature increases, which could result in a foamy rather than creamy texture. Others believe that the choice of wand should adapt to the barista's manual skill.

MILK PITCHERS

A milk pitcher should be made of stainless steel, ideally of 18/10 grade, and must adhere to specific design standards. A skilled barista should have three different-sized pitchers at their disposal.

Stainless steel, particularly the 18/10 grade, is an excellent conductor of heat and allows for easy temperature monitoring by touch. It is also straightforward to clean, highly durable, and aesthetically pleasing. Porcelain, on the other hand, is not recommended due to its insulating properties and fragility.

The design of a milk pitcher is always circular, featuring a narrower top and a spout, which is essential for creating decorative cappuccinos. The bulging lower portion facilitates a specific milk movement that allows it to blend with steam, resulting in a very creamy liquid that doesn't tend to separate.

The recommended capacities for milk pitchers are 16, 23, and 33 fluid ounces (0.5, 0.75, and 1 liter) for preparing two, three, and four cappuccinos at a time without any milk left to reheat. Another important guideline is to never fill a milk pitcher more than half full.

CAPPUCCINO CUP

Just as the espresso cup is of great importance, leading the International Institute of Coffee Tasters to define strict criteria for its material, shape, and size, similar attention should be paid to the cappuccino cup, and its ideal format should be established.

The best material for a cappuccino cup is white feldspathic porcelain. This elegant material doesn't interfere with the visual presentation of the cappuccino and enhances the qualities of a well-prepared one.

The ideal capacity for a cappuccino cup is 5.5 fluid ounces (165 ml), with a tolerance of approximately 10%, which means between 5 and 6 fluid ounces (150–180 ml). This volume consists of 0.8 fluid ounces (25 ml) of espresso and 3.3 fluid ounces (100 ml) of frothed milk, which rises to a volume of about 4.2 fluid ounces (125 ml) when frothed. The cappuccino should be served in a full cup with the frothy layer clearly visible.

Design is also crucial, especially during the pouring of frothed milk when the coffee is incorporated into the milk, creating the perfect ring on the surface of a classic cappuccino. Therefore, the base of the cup should be oval, with varying thickness levels. The cup must have an appropriate diameter and a thin rim to avoid giving the impression of being a cheaply made cup.

METHOD FOR PREPARING A CAPPUCCINO

FROTHING THE MILK

Begin by filling a milk pitcher halfway with cold milk from the refrigerator, ensuring the milk is at a temperature of 38–41 °F (3–5 °C).

Next, turn on the steam function to eliminate any condensation within the steam wand. Once this is done, you can begin the milk frothing process. There are various techniques to consider, depending on several factors, including the volume of steam, the depth to which the wand is submerged in the milk, the angle of immersion in relation to the vertical position of the milk pitcher, and the movements you employ.

Some baristas prefer the following technique: immerse the wand halfway into the milk, apply maximum steam, then immediately raise the nozzle almost to the milk's surface, and finally, plunge it down again to conclude the frothing process.

Others recommend an alternative approach: keep the nozzle near the milk's surface right from the beginning. Position it near the pitcher's brim at an appropriate angle that generates a consistent swirling motion in the milk. To finish, perform a brief plunge of the nozzle to almost the bottom of the milk pitcher.

It's essential to remember that any technique can be considered valid if it results in a uniform "cream" without bubbles. During this phase, your sense of hearing can be quite helpful: pay attention to hissing and gurgling sounds as they can provide important cues about the progress of the frothing process.

ADDING THE MILK TO THE COFFEE

If milk has been frothed correctly, it will maintain its integrity and not separate easily. Therefore, there's no need to rush when using frothed milk. In fact, a brief pause can enhance the texture of the frothed milk, making it smoother, and allowing any foam bubbles on the surface to dissipate. This eliminates the necessity of tapping the milk pitcher on the counter, a practice that professional baristas generally frown upon.

With this in mind, you have ample time to prepare your cappuccino. For a classic cappuccino, position the milk pitcher very close to the cup, and gently pour the frothed milk down the side, allowing the coffee to create the characteristic brown border. If you're making a decorated cappuccino, pour the frothed milk into the center of the cup, starting with the nozzle close to the coffee and gradually moving it away, using your wrist skillfully to create the desired design.

It's crucial to inquire whether the customer desires cocoa before adding the milk. If cocoa is requested, sprinkle it over the coffee. The same principle applies to sugar: some baristas add sugar to the coffee, enabling customers to enjoy the cappuccino as served, without disturbing its overall appearance by stirring.

SERVING COFFEE

A skilled barista takes pride in serving a cappuccino without any spillage. For customers, it can be quite frustrating to find some of their cappuccino in the saucer, making it challenging to enjoy the beverage without getting messy. Timing is crucial when serving a cappuccino, with purists suggesting that it should be consumed within 30 seconds of preparation. However, any delay can compromise the experience, including temperature, which plays a significant role in the initial olfactory impression and overall enjoyment. A cappuccino that's too cold is unappealing, but one that's scalding hot can also be problematic, as it forces the consumer to take tiny sips, reducing the overall pleasantness of the experience.

COFFEE AND MILK

MACCHIATO COFFEE
SERVES 4

INGREDIENTS
4 CUPS OF ESPRESSO COFFEE
1.3 FL OZ (40 ML) FRESH FULL FAT MILK

PREPARATION

- Add about 0.3 fl oz (10 ml) of milk to a cup of espresso. There are three options: the milk can be either cold, hot, or even frothed as for cappuccino.

The original recipe does not include any addition, but a macchiato can be served with a cocoa or cinnamon powder decoration to make the beverage more delicious.

COFFEE AFFOGATO (DROWNED IN COFFEE)
SERVES 4

INGREDIENTS
4 TSP INSTANT COFFEE
2 TSP SUGAR
CREAM, PISTACHIO OR CINNAMON GELATO TO TASTE

PREPARATION

- In a cocktail shaker or a glass jar, combine 4 demitasse cups of hot water with the instant coffee and sugar.
- Close the lid tightly and shake vigorously until a 0.3-inch (1 cm) froth forms on the surface.
- Taste the dessert and add another teaspoon of sugar if it's not sweet enough. Keep in mind that the gelato will also add sweetness.
- Place 2 scoops of gelato into each cup and pour the hot coffee over it.
- Serve immediately. Enjoy!

"Coffee affogato, which literally means 'drowned in coffee,' is a delightful and refreshing dessert that serves as the perfect conclusion to a meal, whether it's the heat of summer or the chill of winter. You can craft affogato using any variety of creamy gelato, except for intensely flavored chocolate gelato. Another excellent choice is stracciatella (chocolate chip) gelato, where fine chocolate shavings delicately enhance the coffee's flavor without overpowering it."

LICORICE WHITE
SERVES 4

INGREDIENTS
3.3-4 FL OZ (100-120 ML) LUNGO ESPRESSO COFFEE
1.4 OZ (40 G) WHITE CHOCOLATE
4 TSP LICORICE
0.6 FL OZ (20 ML) LIQUID SUGAR
20 CRUSHED ICE CUBES

PREPARATION

- Prepare the espresso and preheat four tall cups, keeping them warm, for example, by placing them in a bain-marie away from the flame. Ensure the inside of the cups stays dry.
- Finely chop the white chocolate and place it in a glass to melt.
- Repeat the melting process with the licorice.
- Pour the melted white chocolate into the preheated cups or glasses, followed by the licorice to create two distinct color layers.
- In a frothing jug, combine the ice, liquid sugar, and half of the coffee. Whisk the ingredients using a milk frother or a regular whisk until a soft froth forms.
- Gently pour the remaining coffee over the layers of chocolate and licorice, then top it off delicately with the froth. Serve immediately.

This unique beverage will surprise you with its mosaic of different flavors: the richness coffee, the sweet mellowness of white chocolate, and the fragrant vibrancy of licorice.

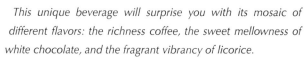

CAFFELATTE
SERVES 4

INGREDIENTS
4 FL OZ (120 ML) ESPRESSO COFFEE
• 27 FL OZ (800 ML) FULL FAT FRESH MILK • SUGAR TO TASTE

PREPARATION

- Heat the milk in a suitably sized jug.
- Make espresso coffee using a moka pot or coffee pods.
- Pour the milk into four cups and then add the coffee.
- Add sugar to taste and serve.

Caffelatte is the typical breakfast beverage, a ritual to kick off the day loved by children and grownups alike. Unlike cappuccino, caffelatte does not have the froth and it usually comes in larger servings. Perfect for dunking cookies, cereals, and fibers.

COFFEE MILK SHAKE
SERVES 4

INGREDIENTS
10 OZ (300 G) OF EITHER COFFEE, CREAM OR VANILLA GELATO •
1.6 FL OZ (50 ML) COLD COFFEE • 12 CRUSHED ICE CUBES •
2 TBSP SUGAR • 16.9 FL OZ (0.5 L) FRESH MILK

PREPARATION

- Crush the ice and place it in the mixer. Add the cold coffee, milk, gelato and sugar.
- Mix for about 3 minutes until frothy.
- Pour into the single glasses and serve.

A coffee milk shake is a classic summer drink: fresh, tasty and irresistible. Easy to prepare, you can also make it with leftover coffee or by replacing the gelato with 3.3 fl oz (100 ml) of very cold whipping cream.

LATTE MACCHIATO THE GERMAN WAY
SERVES 4

INGREDIENTS
4 CUPS OF ESPRESSO COFFEE • 4 GLASSES OF FRESH MILK

PREPARATION

- Heat the milk without bringing it to a boil.
- Froth half of the milk until you obtain a soft frothy texture.
- Pour some of the froth into a glass while making it swirl.
  Leave it to cool down. Add the hot milk.
- Make the espresso coffees and pour them over the milk mixing well.
- Top with the remaining froth.

LATTE MACCHIATO (COFFEE-STAINED MILK)
SERVES 4

INGREDIENTS
4 CUPS OF ESPRESSO COFFEE • 4 GLASSES OF FRESH MILK •
SUGAR AND EXTRACTS (VANILLA, ALMOND) TO TASTE

PREPARATION

- Heat the milk without bringing it to a boil.
- Froth some of the milk until you get a soft cream. Add the sugar or
  the extracts to taste and set aside.
- Pour the milk into a tall tumbler making it quickly swirl and leave it
  to cool a little.
- Make the cups of espresso coffee and pour them slowly into the milk,
- stirring well. Incorporate the froth you had set aside.
- If you are feeling creative, you can add a few drops of coffee on top to
  create a decoration using any sharp kitchen implement.

*Latte macchiato basically inverts the coffee/milk ratio of caffè macchiato.
Latte macchiato is a way of quenching your need of coffee, allowing you
to enjoy perhaps another espresso during the day.*

MAROCCHINO COFFEE
SERVES 4

INGREDIENTS
3.3 FL OZ (100 ML) ESPRESSO COFFEE
2 FL OZ (60 ML) HOT CHOCOLATE
3.3 FL OZ (100 ML) FRESH FULL FAT MILK
COCOA POWDER TO TASTE
SUGAR TO TASTE

PREPARATION

- Let the hot chocolate cool down, then pour it into the glasses.
- Heat the milk without allowing it to boil.
- Prepare the espresso coffee and pour it over the hot chocolate. Sprinkle a little cocoa powder on top.
- Froth the milk in a jug using a milk frother or a mixer, then add it to the coffee. Sprinkle a bit more cocoa powder and serve.
- If you have an espresso machine with a steam wand, you can also froth the milk using it. If you prefer a slightly sweeter dessert, you can add a few teaspoons of sugar and stir.

A cup of Marocchino coffee is also a visual experience. This beverage is typically served in a transparent cup that lets you see the different layers and anticipate their flavors: the chocolate base, the coffee with its cocoa powder topping, and the final milk froth layer chromatically and deliciously crowning the composition.

TURKISH COFFEE
SERVES 4

INGREDIENTS
6.7 FL OZ (200 ML) OF WATER
5 TSP OF COFFEE POWDER
SUGAR TO TASTE
CARDAMOM, CINNAMON OR NUTMEG TO TASTE

PREPARATION

- To make a good Turkish coffee, it's best to begin with Arabica coffee beans and grind them into a fine powder, similar to cocoa powder, using either a grinding machine or a pestle and mortar. This finely ground coffee will bring out the true aroma and enhance your overall coffee preparation experience.
- Here's a step-by-step guide:
- Pour approximately 1.6 fl oz (50 ml) of water into the cezve for each cup you plan to make.
- Add sugar and spices to the cezve, and stir well to combine.
- For each cup you intend to serve, add 1 tsp of coffee plus one extra tsp.
- Place the cezve on gentle heat and bring it to a boil, being careful not to let the foam spill over. Once it starts to boil, remove it from the heat and pour half a cup of coffee and some froth into each serving cup. Return the cezve to the heat source. When the coffee begins to boil again, fill up each cup by pouring the coffee in a lateral motion to maintain the froth. Before serving, add one tablespoon of cold water to help settle the coffee powder at the bottom of each cup.

Turkish coffee is more than just a beverage; it's a cultural icon that embodies the sense of hospitality in a country that has long served as a bridge between the East and the West. This cherished drink is an integral part of everyday life in Turkey and is also featured in important family occasions. For instance, when a young man and his father visit a young woman's parents to propose marriage, cups of Turkish coffee are often served before the conversation begins. It's worth noting that coffee prepared in the Turkish style is also popular in various Middle Eastern countries and Greece. To make this unique coffee, you'll need a special long-handled jug made of copper or brass, known as a cezve.

COFFEE AND MILK

BICERIN
SERVES 6

INGREDIENTS
6.7 FL OZ (200 ML) ESPRESSO COFFEE
2 TBS OF SUGAR
7 OZ (200 G) DARK CHOCOLATE
1.6 FL OZ (50 ML) FRESH WHIPPING CREAM
1.6 FL OZ (50 ML) MILK

PREPARATION

- To prepare a delicious bicerin coffee, follow these steps:
- Make a high-quality espresso coffee and add some sugar to taste. Keep it warm.
- In a separate pot, melt the sugar over gentle heat to create a syrup.
- Place the whipping cream in a bowl and add the sugar syrup. Whisk manually until you achieve a semi-firm, soft, velvety texture.
- Finely chop the chocolate and melt it using a bain-marie or microwave.
- Gradually add part of the milk and the whipped cream mixture to the melted chocolate. Stir and blend thoroughly.
- Combine a bit of chocolate with the remaining whipped cream and set it aside.
- Fill each bicerin cup halfway with the chocolate mixture. Pour the warm espresso coffee over the chocolate and stir well to blend all the flavors.
- Top each cup with the cream and chocolate mixture until it reaches the brim.
- Serve the bicerin coffee hot and savor its delicious taste. Enjoy!

Bicerin, which translates to "small glass" in the Piedmont dialect, is a traditional non-alcoholic beverage from Turin. It has its origins in the eighteenth-century drink known as "bavareisa," which consisted of coffee, chocolate, and frothed milk or whipping cream. Bicerin is a delightful indulgence that harmoniously combines the rich flavors of coffee, chocolate, and milk, resulting in a truly delicious treat.

COFFEE À LA RUSSE
SERVES 4

INGREDIENTS
4 CUPS OF HOT COFFEE • 8 TBSP OF COFFEE LIQUOR •
6.7 FL OZ (2 DL) VODKA • SUGAR TO TASTE

PREPARATION

- Prepare the coffee and pour it into the glasses. In each glass, add sugar to taste and 2 tbsp of coffee liquor. Then, add the vodka, stir well, and serve.

This alcoholic beverage is best enjoyed during the winter. If you prefer a thicker consistency, you can add a small amount of condensed milk and stir it in at the end of the preparation.

THE SULTAN'S COFFEE
SERVES 4

INGREDIENTS
27 FL OZ (8 DL) BOILING COFFEE • 4.5 OZ (130 G) DARK CHOCOLATE • SUGAR OR HONEY TO
TASTE • 12 TBSP OF WHIPPING CREAM • CINNAMON POWDER OR ORANGE ZEST

PREPARATION

- Break up the chocolate and let it melt in a bain-marie. Add sugar to taste and stir it in, then pour the mixture into four transparent glasses. Whisk half of the coffee until frothy and set it aside. Pour a small amount of whipping cream into each glass, then slowly pour in the liquid coffee and its froth. Whip the remaining cream until stiff and add some to each glass. Finally, top with a sprinkle of cinnamon.

CUBAN COFFEE
SERVES 2

INGREDIENTS
1 TSP OF BROWN SUGAR • 2.5 TSP OF COFFEE POWDER • 0.6 FL OZ (20 ML) DARK CUBAN RUM •
1 STRIP OF LEMON ZEST

PREPARATION

- Prepare the moka pot by filling the lower chamber with water.
  Mix the sugar and coffee powder together, then place the mixture
  into the filter without pressing it down. Put the moka pot over
  gentle heat and remove it as soon as the coffee has risen.
  Pour the coffee into the cups, add the rum, decorate with lemon
  zest, and savor the fabulous aroma.

*Cuban coffee is a beverage known for its distinctive and intense sweetness,
attributed to the brown sugar and rum used in its preparation. While the ideal
coffee for this recipe is Cuban coffee, any type of Arabica coffee will suffice.*

MEXICAN COFFEE
SERVES 4

INGREDIENTS
1.6 FL OZ (50 ML) DOUBLE CREAM • 0.1 OZ (4 G) CINNAMON •
A PINCH (1 G) NUTMEG • 0.5 OZ (15 G) SUGAR • 2 ½ CUPS OF BOILING HOT COFFEE •
8 TSP OF CHOCOLATE SYRUP

PREPARATION

- Combine the double cream with 1/3 of the cinnamon in a
  bowl. Mix in the nutmeg and sugar, whisking until the
  mixture thickens.
- To create the base, place 2 teaspoons of chocolate syrup in
  each glass. Add the coffee and stir thoroughly to blend
  the flavors.
- Incorporate the remaining cinnamon into the whipped cream and
  pour the mixture into the glasses.

PARISIAN COFFEE
SERVES 2

INGREDIENTS
2 DEMITASSES OF STRONG COFFEE • 1 DEMITASSES OF HOT CHOCOLATE •
2 TSP COGNAC • SUGAR TO TASTE • 1 FL OZ (30 ML) WHIPPED CREAM

PREPARATION

- Pour ¾ of the coffee and an equal amount of hot chocolate into two small glass cups and stir. Add the cognac and sugar to taste. Then, incorporate the remaining coffee mixed with a little whipped cream. Pour this mixture into the cups and serve, adding a few teaspoons of whipped cream.

SHAKERATO COFFEE
SERVES 2

INGREDIENTS
4 CUPS OF STRONG ESPRESSO • 2 TBSP CRUSHED ICE •
2 TSP SUGAR SYRUP

PREPARATION

- Pour the coffee, syrup, and crushed ice into a shaker. Shake vigorously for at least one minute and serve in ice-cold glasses.

Shakerato coffee is a delicious summer drink, providing a pleasant and refreshing break during the hot hours of the day.

VALDOSTANO COFFEE
SERVES 6

INGREDIENTS
6 CUPS OF STRONG COFFEE
6 SHOT GLASSES OF GRAPPA
6 SHOT GLASSES OF RED WINE
2 SHOT GLASSES OF GENEPÌ LIQUOR
1 ORGANIC LEMON ZEST
12 TSP OF SUGAR

PREPARATION

- Put the sugar in the grole and add the hot coffee, the grappa, the red wine, the genepì, and the grated lemon zest. Heat the grole bain-marie or use steam from an espresso machine. When hot, sprinkle the spouts with some sugar that will caramelize with the heat, acquiring a special flavor.
- The grole is passed to every member of the group who must take a sip of Valdostano coffee from their spout. The quantity should allow for several turns. Groles are made for drinking with friends, since in Val D'Aosta they say that those who drink alone will choke.

Valdostano coffee, literally "coffee of the Val D'Aosta region," requires a grole or coupe de l'amitié, which is a carved wooden bowl with four spouts. It is typically used to drink coffee with a group of friends, emphasizing the value of friendship and community living.

COFFEE AND MILK

VIENNESE COFFEE
SERVES 4

INGREDIENTS
3.5 OZ (100 G) DARK CHOCOLATE • 4 TBSP WHIPPING CREAM •
2 ½ CUPS OF BOILING HOT COFFEE • 5 FL OZ (150 ML) DOUBLE CREAM •
1 TSP SUGAR

PREPARATION

- Melt the chocolate in a small pot and pour it into
  four hot glasses.
- Slowly add the coffee and the tablespoons of whipping
  cream, whisking well until frothy and keep warm.
- Whip the double cream and sugar, and garnish by adding
  a few tablespoons of whipped double cream to each glass.

MARTINI COFFEE
SERVES 4

INGREDIENTS
4 CUPS OF STRONG ESPRESSO • 4 TBSP OF SUGAR
• 4 FL OZ (120 ML) VODKA • SOME CRUSHED ICE •
FINELY GRATED CHOCOLATE

PREPARATION

- Pour coffee, sugar, vodka and ice into the shaker. Shake well.
- Filter and pour into each glass. Garnish with a sprinkle of grated chocolate.

COFFEE AND MILK

EXTRA STRONG COFFEE GRANITA
SERVES 2

INGREDIENTS
4 CUPS STRONG COFFEE
2 CUPS SUGAR
2 GLASSES KAHLÚA (MEXICAN COFFEE LIQUOR)
2 GLASSES DARK RUM
2 CUPS CRUSHED ICE
8 TBSP HONEY

PREPARATION

- Mix sugar, honey, and the liquors in a metal container. Add the cold coffee and place it in the freezer for one hour.
- Scrape the icy mixture with a fork to make granita.
- Add the crushed ice and return it to the freezer for another 3 hours, scraping the mixture every hour.
- Place the granita in the serving glasses and enjoy.

COFFEE AND MILK

COFFEE GROG
SERVES 4

INGREDIENTS
12 LUMPS OF SUGAR • 4 STRIPS OF ORGANIC LEMON ZEST •
4 TBSP OF BRANDY (FOR FLAMBÉING) • 4 CUPS ESPRESSO COFFEE

PREPARATION

- Rinse 4 glasses with hot water. Place 4 lumps of sugar in
  every glass and add the lemon zest.
- Add the coffee. Flame the tablespoons of brandy with a lighter
  and add them to the coffee. Serve while still very hot.

The name Grog derives from gros grain *the coarse wool-and-silk fabric
worn by British admiral Edward Vernon who went down in history
for having prohibited spirits to his crew. The only drink they were
allowed was watered down rum to keep them from getting drunk.*

IRISH COFFEE
SERVES 4

INGREDIENTS
4 FL OZ (120 ML) IRISH WHISKEY •
0.5 OZ (15 G) BROWN SUGAR •
10 FL OZ (300 ML) STRONG COFFEE • 1.5 FL OZ (45 ML)
DOUBLE CREAM, LIGHTLY WHIPPED

PREPARATION

- Heat 4 glass cups or 4 tall glasses.
- Dry them inside and pour in the sugar.
- Add the whiskey and then the coffee.
- Stir well until the sugar dissolves. Then add a spoonful of cream and stir.

COFFEE SORBET
SERVES 4

INGREDIENTS
14 OZ (400 G) SUGAR
8.8 OZ (250 G) STRONG COFFEE
8.4 FL OZ (250 ML) WATER
1 EGG WHITE
A LITTLE COFFEE POWDER

PREPARATION

- Add 12 oz (350 g) of sugar to the water. Place it over the heat and boil for one minute.
- Add the coffee and stir well using a whisk.
- Place it in the fridge to cool for a few hours and then pour it into a metal vessel, filtering it with a small colander.
- Beat the egg white and the rest of the sugar until stiff, then delicately add it to the mixture.
- Place it in the freezer for about 6 hours and use a mixer or a whisk to stir it around two or three times so that it remains homogeneous.
- Leave it out of the freezer for about 10 minutes before serving. Serve it in tall, thin glasses and sprinkle with a little coffee powder.

COFFEE AND MILK

20 RECIPES

BY CHEF GIOVANNI RUGGIERI

PAIRING
COFFEE AND FOOD

BEETROOT AND COFFEE SCALLOPS WITH A CHILI AND DARK COCOA SAUCE

SERVES 4

12 SCALLOPS
1 OZ (30 G) CLARIFIED BUTTER
3.5 OZ (100 G) VACUUM PACKED COOKED BEETROOT
0.7 OZ (20 G) EXTRA VIRGIN OLIVE OIL
0.1 OZ (4 G) COFFEE POWDER
0.2 OZ (8 G) COCOA POWDER
3.5 OZ (100 G) CHOPPED TOMATOES
1 SHALLOT
0.1 OZ (5 G) CONCENTRATED TOMATO PUREE
0.3 OZ (10 G) WHITE VINEGAR
1 OZ (30 G) CASTER SUGAR
0.1 OZ (5 G) SOY SAUCE
3 RED HOT CHILI PEPPERS
0.7 OZ (20 G) SESAME OIL
SALT TO TASTE

PREPARATION TIME: 30 MINUTES

Julienne the chili peppers and the shallot, and brown them in the sesame oil. Add the concentrated tomato puree, chopped tomatoes, a little salt, soy sauce, vinegar, sugar, and cook for about 1 hour over low heat until you obtain a thick sauce. Mix it to make it nice and smooth and leave it to cool. Filter it with a colander. Peel the beetroot and blend it, adding 1.7 oz (50 g) of water, the olive oil, and a pinch of salt. Keep the cream warm in a bain-marie.

Using a spoon, separate the scallops from the shells. Rinse them under running water, delicately remove the coral pulp and the stomach. Dry them on some absorbent paper, transfer them onto a plate, and sprinkle some salt on top.

Put the butter in a pan over high heat and brown three scallops at a time on each side so that the cooking temperature remains constant. Rapidly brown the coral pulp too (2 minutes).

Irregularly display the beetroot cream and the chili sauce, adding the scallops and sprinkling the coffee and cocoa powder on top. Serve hot.

BRAISED ARTICHOKES AND JERUSALEM ARTICHOKES CREAMED WITH PARMIGIANO REGGIANO CHEESE WITH A TOUCH OF COFFEE

SERVES 4

4 ARTICHOKES
4 MEDIUM-SIZE JERUSALEM ARTICHOKES
1 LEMON
0.3 FL OZ (10 ML) WHITE WINE
0.3 OZ (10 G) WHITE VINEGAR
10.5 OZ (300 G) GRATED PARMIGIANO
REGGIANO CHEESE
3.5 OZ (100 G) WHIPPING CREAM

10.5 OZ (300 G) MILK
1 OZ (30 G) ESPRESSO COFFEE
0.3 OZ (9 G) AGAR-AGAR
2.4 OZ (70 G) BUTTER
0.3 OZ (9 G) UNREFINED BROWN SUGAR
SALT AND PEPPER TO TASTE
EXTRA VIRGIN OLIVE OIL TO TASTE
COFFEE POWDER TO GARNISH

PREPARATION TIME: 1 HOUR

Place a bain-marie pot over low heat. Pour in the cream, butter, and parmigiano reggiano cheese until you obtain a fondue. Then use an immersion blender to make the cream perfectly smooth.

Pour the milk in equal quantities into three different pots. In each pot, add a different quantity of coffee: 0.1 oz (5 g) in the first, 0.3 oz (10 g) in the second, and 0.5 oz (15 g) in the third. Add the sugar, stir, and bring to a boil. Leave to cool, add 0.1 oz (3 g) of agar-agar in each pot, whisk, and bring to a boil. Leave to cool for 3 hours until the sauces become firm.

Use an immersion blender to mix them into a fluid cream.

Remove the artichokes' hard outer leaves, trim the thorny tips, and peel the stalks. Cut the artichokes in half, remove the choke with a small knife, and place in a bowl of cold water with some lemon juice. Peel the jerusalem artichokes and add them to the lemony water too.

Fill a saucepan with enough water to cook the jerusalem artichokes, add salt and the vinegar and cook over low heat until soft, but not overcooked. Drain the jerusalem artichokes, cut the ends, and use a ring mold to shape them into small cylinders. Cut them into approximately 0.7 in (2 cm) discs.

Pour some oil in a non-stick pan and stir fry the artichokes for 3 minutes over high heat. Add salt and pepper, add the wine and let it evaporate. Then put the lid on and leave to cook until all the liquid has evaporated.

Place the three coffee sauces on the plate, put the hot vegetables on top and pour over the hot parmigiano reggiano fondue. Garnish with coffee powder before serving.

COFFEE-SMOKED VEAL FILLET WITH COCOA BEAN IN BALSAMIC VINEGAR SWEET-AND-SOUR SAUCE AND SWEET POTATO CHIPS

SERVES 4

14 OZ (400 G) VEAL FILLET
3.5 OZ (100 G) COFFEE BEANS
3.5 OZ (100 G) BEECH WOOD CHIPS FOR SMOKING
1 COCOA BEAN
2 ORANGE SWEET POTATOES
13.5 FL OZ (400 ML) CORN OIL FOR FRYING
5.2 OZ (150 G) BALSAMIC VINEGAR
1.7 OZ (50 G) UNREFINED BROWN SUGAR
10 BLACK PEPPERCORNS
SALT AND PEPPER TO TASTE
EXTRA VIRGIN OLIVE OIL TO TASTE

PREPARATION TIME: 45 MINUTES

Preheat the oven to 195 °f (90 °c). Place the smoking wood chips in a 5.9 in (15 cm) non-stick pan with a steam-cooking grill. Set the wood chips alight until they burn completely, then sprinkle the coffee beans on top. Place the fillet on the grill, cover it with the lid and place it in the oven for 30 minutes. Brush the meat with olive oil, letting it brown on both sides in the non-stick pan, and grate the cocoa bean while turning the meat on both sides. Add salt and pepper.

Pour vinegar, sugar, and pepper in a pot and place it over low heat until they thicken into a sauce. Remove the peppercorns using a colander.

Heat the corn oil in a deep frying pan. Wash and dry the potatoes. With a mandoline slicer, cut them into about 1mm slices. Fry the potatoes in the hot oil without letting the slices overlap. Shake the pan so that the slices fry evenly. When ready, remove the chips from the pan and transfer them onto some absorbent paper. Add more potatoes to the oil. Continue like this until all the potatoes are ready.

Cut the fillet into 4 slices and place each slice onto the plates. Pour some sweet-and-sour sauce, add a few chips on the side and serve.

BUTTER AND TARRAGON ESCARGOTS WITH COFFEE AND JUNIPER SAUCE

SERVES 4

24 LUMACHE
24 ESCARGOTS
5.6 OZ (160 G) BUTTER
1.4 OZ (40 G) BREAD CRUMBS
0.3 OZ (10 G) TARRAGON
1.6 FL OZ (50 ML) WHITE WINE
1 OZ (30 G) WHITE VINEGAR
1 GARLIC CLOVE
1 OZ (30 G) SODIUM BICARBONATE TO CLEANSE
THE ESCARGOT SHELLS
SALT AND PEPPER TO TASTE
WATERCRESS SPROUTS TO HAVE ON THE SIDE

FOR THE SAUCE:
1 CELERY STALK • 1 CARROT • 1 ONION •
1 TSP OF TOMATO CONCENTRATE • 1 VEAL
KNEE • 2 PEPPERCORNS • 1 SMALL BAY
LEAF • 3.3 FL OZ (100 ML) WHITE WINE •
0.1 OZ (5 G) POTATO STARCH •
1 OZ (30 G) CRUSHED COFFEE BEANS •
2 CRUSHED JUNIPER BERRIES • EXTRA VIRGIN
OLIVE OIL TO TASTE

PREPARATION TIME, COOKING EXCLUDED: 1 HOUR (at least)

Preheat the oven to 390 °F (200 °C). Grease the veal knee and place it in the oven for about 30 minutes or until it becomes brown. Wash the vegetables, dice them, and brown them in a pan with a little oil. Transfer the browned vegetables to a large saucepan. Add the veal knee, tomato concentrate, bay leaves, and peppercorns. Pour in the wine and simmer until it evaporates. Add some cold water and a few ice cubes, filling the saucepan to the brim, then bring it to a boil over gentle heat. Cook until the broth is reduced by half. Strain the broth through a fine mesh colander. Add the crushed coffee beans and juniper berries to the broth. Return it to the heat and simmer until you are left with a dark and tasty sauce. Strain the sauce once more and set it aside to cool. Fill ¾ of a large saucepan with water, adding 0.5 fl oz (15 g) of vinegar, 0.8 fl oz (25 ml) of wine, and a pinch of salt. Place it over medium heat. When it comes to a boil, add the escargots with their shells and cook for 60 minutes. Drain the escargots and extract them from their shells. Eliminate the black part of the intestines and wash the escargots under cold running water. Return the escargots to the saucepan and bring them to a boil once more, using the same ingredients, for another 60 minutes. Boil the shells in water and bicarbonate for 10 minutes. Mix and soften the butter, then add the chopped tarragon, breadcrumbs, a crushed garlic clove (without the germ), salt, and freshly ground black pepper. Place the escargots in the shells and seal them with a layer of the herby butter. Put the escargots in the fridge for a few minutes until the butter becomes firm. Return the sauce to the heat and bring it to a boil. Gradually pour in the potato starch while stirring well with a whisk to prevent any lumps. Preheat the oven to 370 °F (190 °C) and bake the escargots for 10 minutes. Then place them on a platter with the sauce and some watercress sprouts on the side.

MARINATED MACKEREL WITH KATSUOBUSHI AND PORCINI MUSHROOM SOUP

SERVES 4

4 MACKEREL FILLETS
1 OZ (30 G) KATSUOBUSHI
3.5 OZ (100 G) MISO PASTE
1 ORGANIC LEMON
1 ORGANIC ORANGE
1 OZ (30 G) COFFEE BEANS
6.7 FL OZ (200 ML) EXTRA VIRGIN OLIVE OIL
2 OZ (60 G) SOY SAUCE
0.7 OZ (20 G) DRY PORCINI MUSHROOMS
0.7 OZ (20 G) WHITE WINE
1 BAY LEAF
1 BUNCH OF PARSLEY
SALT TO TASTE

PREPARATION TIME: 45 MINUTES

Grate the lemon and orange zest and mix it into the miso paste. Use the mixture to cover each mackerel fillet on the meat side. Squeeze half of the lemon and the orange. Pour the juices into one container and mix them together. Place the mackerel fillets in the juice, skin-side down, and leave them to marinate for 12 hours in the fridge.

Rinse the mackerels under running water to remove the miso paste. Pat them dry with some absorbent paper and sprinkle some salt on the meat side. Heat the olive oil in a pan. Place the mackerel fillets skin-side up and then place the pan in the oven preheated to 175 °F (80 °C) for 20 minutes.

Soak the dry porcini mushrooms in warm water for 20 minutes, then drain them, removing any earthy residues. Put the mushrooms in a saucepan with 16 fl oz (500 ml) of water, the wine, soy sauce, bay leaf, crushed coffee beans, and 0.7 oz (20 g) of Katsuobushi. Boil for 5 minutes and then strain.

Pour the hot broth into the bowls and add the mackerels skin-side up. Garnish with a few drops of oil, some parsley leaves, and a few Katsuobushi flakes.

COFFEE LASAGNE WITH PECORINO CHEESE, RICOTTA AND OCTOPUS COOKED IN CURRY SOUP

SERVES 4

14 OZ (400 G) RICOTTA CHEESE
5.2 OZ (150 G) GRATED PECORINO CHEESE
3.5 OZ (100 G) GRATED PARMESAN CHEESE
2.2 LB (1 KG) OCTOPUS
0.3 OZ (10 G) CURRY
1 LEMON
1 CLOVE OF GARLIC
16.9 FL OZ (500 ML) WHIPPING CREAM
1.7 OZ (50 G) BUTTER
14 OZ (400 G) STRONG ALL-PURPOSE FLOUR (FLOUR TYPE 0)
3 LARGE EGGS
0.7 OZ (20 G) FINELY GROUND COFFEE
SALT AND PEPPER TO TASTE
EXTRA VIRGIN OLIVE OIL TO TASTE

PREPARATION TIME: 45 MINUTES

Put the flour, coffee, and eggs into a stand mixer and mix. Wrap the mixture with cling film and put it in the fridge for 30 minutes.

Clean the octopus, leave it in water for 15 minutes, remove the eyes, beak, and innards. Place it in a pan, cover with water, add the curry, lemon cut in half, and the unpeeled garlic clove. Bring to a boil, lower the heat to a gentle simmer for 40 minutes. Drain and leave to cool in ice water. Cut off the ends of the tentacles and set them aside for garnish, then cut the rest of the tentacles into thin rounds. Brown them in a non-stick pan with a little oil. Cut the octopus into rounds as well.

Slice the lasagne mixture and, using a rolling pin, roll the slices to a thickness of 0.05 in (1 mm). Grease the individual molds with butter and brush the sides with a little cream. Cut the pasta to fit the molds and line them. Mix the ricotta with salt and pepper, then alternate the lasagne sheets covered with a layer of ricotta, pecorino cheese, a little octopus, Parmesan cheese, and butter, adding a few teaspoons of cream. Place the tentacle rounds on the last layers. The final layer is covered with butter, cream, and cheeses.

Bake in a preheated oven at 370 °F (190 °C) for 18 minutes, and grill the top cheese layer.

Serve the lasagne hot and garnish with octopus tentacle tips.

PACCHERI STUFFED WITH CLAM MOUSSE INFUSED IN COFFEE WITH PEA CREAM AND SPROUTS

SERVES 4

11.2 OZ (320 G) PACCHERI
4.4 LB (2 KG) CLAMS
3.5 OZ (100 G) SHELLED PEAS
A SMALL BUNCH OF PEA SPROUTS
10 COFFEE BEANS
3.5 OZ (100 G) POTATOES
2 EGG WHITES
5.2 OZ (150 G) WHITE WINE
A FEW PARSLEY LEAVES
SALT
EXTRA VIRGIN OLIVE OIL TO TASTE

PREPARATION TIME: 1 HOUR

Peel the potatoes and cook them in salted water for 40 minutes over low heat.

Wash the clams thoroughly in cold water, agitating them to remove all the sand. Then soak them in a little salty water for 15 minutes. Pour the oil into a pan and sauté the parsley, coffee beans, and drained clams. Add the wine, simmer and reduce, and cover the pan. Cook for 3 minutes after it starts boiling. Allow it to cool at room temperature for a few minutes, then remove the clams from their shells. Strain the cooking liquid and add it to the clams.

Add the cooked potatoes and blend to obtain a soft velouté-like sauce. Add the egg whites and blend again. Strain the mixture and put it into a mousse siphon, then add 2 charges and shake.

Boil the peas in salted water for 2 minutes. Drain and blend them with a little cooking water, salt, and oil until you have a smooth cream. Strain the cream through a strainer.

Cook the paccheri in plenty of salted water, being careful not to break them. Cook for 1-2 minutes less than the recommended time on the package. Drain, place them in a bowl, and drizzle them with oil.

Spoon the pea cream onto the plate, fill each pacchero with the clam mousse, and arrange them on top of the cream to form a small tower. Garnish with pea sprouts.

SUCKLING PIG RAVIOLINI, SEASONED WITH CORIANDER, LEMON, COFFEE POWDER AND MUSTARD SPROUTS

SERVES 4

17 OZ (500 G) FLOUR	3 RADISHES
19 EGG YOLKS	3 EGGS
14 OZ (400 G) SUCKLING PIG SHOULDER	1 TSP TOMATO PASTE
1 SHALLOT	3 LEMONS
1 CARROT	3.5 OZ (100 G) BUTTER
1 CELERY STALK	1 SMALL BUNCH OF MUSTARD SPROUTS
1 BAY LEAF	0.3 OZ (10 G) FINELY GROUND COFFEE
6.7 FL OZ (200 ML) WHITE WINE	SALT AND PEPPER TO TASTE
1 BUNCH CORIANDER	EXTRA VIRGIN OLIVE OIL TO TASTE

PREPARATION TIME: 1 HOUR

Wash and chop the vegetables. Preheat the oven to 360 °F (180 °C). Cut the shoulder into small pieces and brown them in a little oil. Add the chopped vegetables and cook for a few minutes. Incorporate the bay leaf and tomato paste, then deglaze with the wine. Cover and cook in the oven for 1 hour and 30 minutes. If needed, add half a glass of water to prevent the meat from drying out.

Let the meat and vegetables cool, then pass them through a mincer. Add the eggs, grated radishes, chopped coriander, salt, and pepper. Transfer the mixture into a pastry bag.

Mix the flour and egg yolks in a stand mixer until well combined. Wrap the dough in cling film and place it in the fridge for 30 minutes. Roll out the dough to a thickness of 1 mm. Place walnut-sized portions of the meat mixture at regular intervals of 0.7 inches (2 cm) on the pastry, forming two horizontal rows 0.7 inches (2 cm) apart. Fold the pastry borders over the meat and press with your fingers to seal the raviolini. Arrange the finished raviolini on a tray lined with baking paper sprinkled with flour. Continue until you've used all the ingredients, then refrigerate the tray.

In a small pan, melt the butter without allowing it to boil. Add the grated lemon zest. Gradually whisk in 3.5 oz (100 g) of water until a well-blended cream forms. Season with salt and pepper and refrigerate.

Cook the raviolini in salted boiling water for 2 minutes, drain, and place them in a non-stick pan. Toss them with the butter cream, adding a few tablespoons of water if necessary to achieve a shiny appearance.

Serve the raviolini in soup plates, garnish with mustard sprouts, and sprinkle with coffee.

GORGONZOLA RISOTTO AND BRITTLE WITH FINE SAVORY COFFEE CRUMBLE WITH CHARD AND TOMATO POWDER

SERVES 4

1 BUNCH GREEN CHARD (ABOUT 10/12 LEAVES)
3 TOMATOES
12.3 OZ (350 G) CARNAROLI RICE
7 OZ (200 G) SWEET GORGONZOLA
4.2 OZ (120 G) GRATED PARMESAN CHEESE
2.7 FL OZ (80 ML) WHITE WINE
1.7 OZ (50 G) BUTTER
SALT TO TASTE
EXTRA VIRGIN OLIVE OIL TO TASTE

FOR THE BRITTLE:
2 EGG WHITES • 1.7 OZ (50 G) BUTTER • 1.7 OZ (50 G) STRONG ALL-PURPOSE FLOUR (FLOUR TYPE 0) • 0.3 OZ (10 G) INSTANT COFFEE • A PINCH OF SALT

FOR THE FINE COFFEE CRUMBLE:
2.1 OZ (60 G) ALMOND FLOUR • 2.1 OZ (60 G) STRONG ALL-PURPOSE FLOUR (FLOUR TYPE 0) • 4 OZ (115 G) BUTTER • 0.7 OZ (20 G) INSTANT COFFEE • 0.1 OZ (5 G) SUGAR 0.1 OZ (5 G) HONEY

PREPARATION TIME: 45 MINUTES

Wash the tomatoes and score a cross on the bottom of each tomato. Blanch them in plenty of boiling water for 10 seconds, then immediately plunge them into icy water to cool. Peel them, cut them into quarters and remove the seeds. Put the tomatoes in the microwave for 5 minutes at 400 W to dry.

Wash and dry the chards, cut off the stalks. Place each leaf on a plate and put in the microwave for 2 minutes at 400 W. Repeat if the leaf is not tender. Dry all the leaves then crush them and press them through a sieve together with the tomatoes.

For the brittle put room-temperature soft butter in a bowl, add the flour, egg whites, coffee and salt, whisk well until the ingredients take on an even coffee color. Pre-heat oven to 360 °F (180 °C). Cover baking tray with baking paper and place small 0,08 in (2 mm) high 3.9x1.5 in (10x4 cm) strips of cream on the tray. Bake in oven for 8 minutes.

For the fine coffee crumble put the room-temperature softened butter in a bowl with the coffee, sugar, honey and mix and blend well. Add a spoonful at a time of the mixed flours stirring well to obtain a grainy crumbly mixture. Spread onto a baking tray lined with baking paper and bake in the oven at 320 °F (160 °C) for 20 minutes. Every 5 minutes work the mixture to keep it flat, especially at the center so that it bakes evenly. Remove from the oven, let it cool at room temperature, the crumble should now be crunchy.

Pour 2 gal (8 l) of lightly salted water into a large saucepan and bring to the boil. Put 3 tablespoons of oil in another saucepan and brown the rice with a pinch of salt. Stir the rice continually to brown it evenly, deglaze with the wine until completely evaporated. Add a few ladles of boiling water and continue stirring. Cook the rice for 14 minutes adding hot water little by little, do not add too much water, the risotto must be rather dry when cooked. Add the butter, stir, add the gorgonzola and Parmesan cheeses, stir until the risotto becomes creamy.

Spoon the hot rice into the plates, add the tomato and chard powders, the fine coffee crumble and serve. Serve the coffee brittle on the side so it maintains its crispiness.

PUMPKIN AND STAR ANISE VELOUTE SAUCE WITH COFFEE AND RASPBERRY LAYER

SERVES 4

8.8 OZ (250 G) RASPBERRIES
2.0 OZ (80 G) SUGAR
JUICE OF HALF A LEMON
17.6 OZ (500 G) SKINNED AND SEEDED PUMPKIN
1 STAR ANISE
0.7 OZ (20 G) BUTTER
0.1 OZ (5 G) FINELY GROUND COFFEE
SALT TO TASTE
EXTRA VIRGIN OLIVE OIL TO TASTE
GARNISH WITH MARJORAM LEAVES

PREPARATION TIME: 30 MINUTES

Whisk the raspberries with the lemon juice and strain the mixture to eliminate the seeds. Add the sugar and boil until it's reduced to jam. Spread the mixture on a silpat baking sheet. Preheat the oven to 170 °F (75 °C) and bake for 3 hours.

Pour 13.5 fl oz (400 ml) of water into a saucepan, add the star anise, and boil for 5 minutes. Cut the pumpkin into small pieces and cook in the butter for 5 minutes. Strain the water and star anise, then add it to the pumpkin. Season with a little salt and cook covered on low heat for 30 minutes. Cool and then blend to get a shiny, smooth velvet sauce.

Serve the hot velvet sauce in transparent bowls, sprinkle some coffee powder, and cover it with the raspberry layer cut into a circle. Garnish with fresh marjoram leaves and drizzle with a bit of oil.

BROWNED DUCK WITH RED CABBAGE, COFFEE AVOCADO WITH A SCENT OF CUMIN

SERVES 4

2 WHOLE DUCK BREASTS	1.7 OZ (50 G) EXTRA VIRGIN OLIVE OIL
1 RED CABBAGE	0.1 OZ (5 G) CUMIN SEEDS
AGAR-AGAR	0.3OZ (10 G) SOY LECITHIN
RED WINE VINEGAR	3.5 OZ (100 G) CLARIFIED BUTTER
3 RIPE AVOCADOS	4 SAGE LEAVES
0.1 OZ (3 G) INSTANT COFFEE	1 ROSEMARY TWIG
½ LEMON JUICE	SALT AND PEPPER TO TASTE

PREPARATION TIME: 45 MINUTES

Wash and cut the cabbage into pieces, removing the central core. Place it in a blender and add 0.1 oz (2 g) of agar-agar for every 3.5 oz (100 g) of juice. Mix well with a whisk and bring to a boil. Let it cool for 3 hours in the fridge. Blend the juice until creamy, pass it through a sieve, and add a little salt, 2 tablespoons of oil, and 0.1 oz (3 g) of vinegar for every 3.3 fl oz (100 ml) of cream.

Cut the avocados in half and remove the skin. Place the pulp in a bowl and mash until you have a chunky cream. Add the remaining oil, salt, lemon juice, and coffee, and mix well.

Boil 17 fl oz (500 ml) of water with the cumin seeds for 10 minutes on low heat. Filter and let it cool. Add the soy lecithin and blend to create a very thick foam.

Separate the duck breasts and make square-like incisions into the skin with a knife. Sprinkle salt and pepper on both sides. Heat a non-stick pan and brown the breasts on the skin side without adding any oil. Brown on the other side for 2 minutes over medium heat, adding butter, sage, and rosemary. Place in the oven heated to 370 °F(190 °C) for 5 minutes.

Cut the meat into regular slices and absorb the blood with kitchen paper. Serve the meat on a thin layer of cabbage cream with some avocado cream and a spoonful of cumin foam on the side. Add a little ground coffee to decorate the dish.

BOAR MORSEL COOKED IN WINE
WITH CHOCOLATE
AND COFFEE EGGPLANTS

SERVES 4

28 OZ (800 G) BOAR LEG	1 ROSEMARY TWIG
1 CELERY STALK	3 BLACK PEPPERCORNS
1 CARROT	3 JUNIPER BERRIES
1 ONION	1 TSP OF CONCENTRATED TOMATO PUREE
2 GARLIC CLOVES	1 OZ (30 G) BALSAMIC VINEGAR
3.5 OZ (100 G) BUTTER	4 EGGPLANTS
1.7 OZ (50 G) WHITE GRAPPA	4.2 OZ (120 G) 72% DARK CHOCOLATE
1.7 OZ (50 G) CHERRY LIQUOR	0.1 OZ (3 G) INSTANT COFFEE
33 FL OZ (1 L) RED WINE	SALT AND PEPPER TO TASTE
1 BAY LEAF	EXTRA VIRGIN OLIVE OIL TO TASTE

PREPARATION TIME: 45 MINUTES

Dice the boar leg into 2-inch (5 cm) cubes, add salt and pepper, and brown them on each side with the butter and 3 tablespoons of oil. Finely dice the celery, carrot, and onion. Put the vegetables to brown in a large pot with a little oil. Add salt, pepper, rosemary, bay leaf, peppercorns, and juniper berries. Let them brown until caramelized. Add the well-browned boar.

Add a little wine to the meat juices and let it evaporate. With a wooden spoon, gently scrape the bottom of the saucepan so that the caramelization gives flavor to the wine. Pour the remaining wine and meat juice onto the meat, add 2 glasses of water and the tomato paste. Put the lid on and cook over very low heat for 2 hours, with the garlic, taking care to keep the meat always moist.

Wash the eggplants and cut them into 4 lengthwise. Cook them in the oven at 360 °F (180 °C) for 45 minutes.

Add the vinegar, cherry liquor, and grappa to the meat and continue cooking for another 40 minutes until tender.

Place the meat on a serving dish and filter the cooking juices with a fine-mesh strainer; also squash the vegetables with a spoon to extract all the flavor and then return everything to the heat to thicken the sauce.

Before serving, heat the eggplant pulp again. Add a pinch of salt and 2 tablespoons of oil.

Melt the chocolate in a bain-marie, add the coffee and mix well.

Arrange the meat on one side of each plate, the eggplant on the other, and pour some chocolate and coffee sauce on top.

BEEF SIRLOIN WITH COFFEE POWDER, CHICORY, CAPERS AND CHILI PEPPER

SERVES 4

28 OZ (800 G) BEEF SIRLOIN
0.1 OZ (3 G) FINELY GROUND COFFEE
28.2 OZ (800 G) CHICORY OR PUNTARELLE
15 CAPER BERRIES
2 CHILI PEPPERS
1 GARLIC CLOVE
SALT AND PEPPER TO TASTE
EXTRA VIRGIN OLIVE OIL TO TASTE

PREPARATION TIME: 30 MINUTES

Wash the puntarelle and cut off the shoots of the sprouts, separating them from the smaller and tender leaves. Eliminate the larger leaves.

Blanch the leaves and the chicory in plenty of salted water for 3 minutes, drain, and cool in cold water and ice.

Cut 4 slices of sirloin about 1-1.4 inches (3-4 cm) thick and add salt and pepper. Pour 3 tablespoons of oil into a non-stick pan. When hot, add the meat and brown it. Then transfer the meat to the oven – pre-heated to 390 °F (200 °C) – and roast it for another 4 minutes.

In another saucepan, pour a little oil with the unpeeled garlic clove, minced capers, and red pepper; brown for 2 minutes on low heat.

Incorporate the blanched puntarelle without making them brown. Add some salt and sprinkle with coffee.

Cut the meat into small pieces, placing them next to the puntarelle. Serve while still hot.

LAMB CUTLETS WITH COFFEE, BLACK PEPPER AND GINGER BREADCRUMB COATING WITH WATERCRESS SALAD

SERVES 4

28.8 OZ (800 G) FRENCHED LAMB SIRLOIN
14 OZ (400 G) PANKO (JAPANESE BREADCRUMBS)
0.7 OZ (20 G) FINELY GROUND COFFEE
4 CRUSHED BLACK PEPPERCORNS
0.1 OZ (20 G) FRESH GINGER
4 EGGS
1.7 OZ (50 G) MILK
5.2 OZ (150 G) STRONG ALL-PURPOSE FLOUR (FLOUR TYPE 0)
10 FL OZ (300 ML) CORN OIL FOR FRYING
1.7 OZ (50 G) CLARIFIED BUTTER
2 BUNCHES OF WATERCRESS
2 LIMES
SALT FLAKES TO TASTE
EXTRA VIRGIN OLIVE OIL TO TASTE

PREPARATION TIME: 45 MINUTES

Cut the meat into 0.7-inch (2 cm) thick slices. Lightly grease them with oil and place them between two sheets of wax paper. Use a meat mallet to reduce their thickness to 0.2 inches (0.5 cm) and sprinkle some salt on both sides.

Mix the panko with the crushed peppercorns, grated ginger, and coffee powder.

Beat the eggs with the milk in a large bowl.

Coat the slices of meat with some flour, dip them in the eggs, and then coat them with the panko mixture.

Put the butter and the corn oil in a frying pan and fry two slices at a time until golden. Drain them on kitchen paper.

Wash the watercress, removing the larger leaves, and set aside the whole sprouts for the salad.

Dry the leaves with kitchen paper and dress them with the juice of one lime and the grated zest of the two limes.

Add extra virgin olive oil and salt.

Serve the cutlets on a single platter with the bones on the same side and the salad next to them.

COFFEE MARINATED TUNA WITH EMBER-COOKED CARROTS AND SHISO LEAVES IN COFFEE AND SESAME TEMPURA

SERVES 4

25.3 OZ (720 G) ATLANTIC BLUEFIN TUNA
0.7 OZ (20 G) COFFEE BEANS
1.7 OZ (50 G) SOY SAUCE
0.3 OZ (10 G) RICE VINEGAR
1.7 OZ (50 G) BROWN SUGAR
8 CARROTS WITH THEIR TOPS
16 SHISO LEAVES
0.2 OZ (6 G) FINELY GROUND COFFEE
0.3 OZ (10 G) WHITE SESAME
1.7 OZ (50 G) RICE FLOUR
1.7 OZ (50 G) STRONG ALL-PURPOSE FLOUR (FLOUR TYPE 0)
A PINCH (2 G) OF INSTANT COFFEE
1 BOTTLE OF 17 FL OZ (500 ML) SPARKLING WATER
10 OZ (300 G) PEANUT OIL

PREPARATION TIME: 30 MINUTES

In a saucepan, pour 17 fl oz (500 ml) of water, and add the coffee beans, vinegar, soy sauce, and sugar. Bring to a boil and let it simmer for 3 minutes. Filter the mixture and set it aside to cool.

Slice the tuna into approximately 1-inch (3 cm) thick pieces and place them in the cold vinegar and coffee marinade for 3 hours.

Combine the flours, sesame seeds, and instant coffee. Slowly pour in the cold sparkling water from the fridge while stirring. Whisk until you achieve a creamy tempura batter that is neither too thick nor too runny. Refrigerate the batter to keep it cool.

Peel and wash the carrots, leaving the green tops intact. Wrap each carrot in aluminum foil and cook them over the embers of a barbecue grill for 5 minutes on each side. Remove the tuna from the marinade and pat it dry with kitchen paper. Heat the peanut oil to 360 °F (180 °C). Whisk the tempura batter and dip the shiso leaves in it. Fry them one at a time for about 1 minute each until they become crispy. Pat them dry with kitchen paper. Quickly sear the tuna in a very hot nonstick pan for a few seconds on each side, leaving it rare in the center but not cold. Remove the foil from the carrots. To serve, place one carrot on each plate, along with some shiso leaves. Arrange the diagonally cut tuna on the side without letting the ingredients touch. Serve promptly.

CHOCOLATE DEMI-SPHÈRE WITH COFFEE MOUSSE AND FINE COFFEE CRUMBLE

SERVES 4

FOR THE CHOCOLATE DEMI-SPHÈRE:
10 OZ (300 G) 72% DARK CHOCOLATE

FOR THE COFFEE MOUSSE:
14 OZ (400 G) WHIPPING CREAM
0.5 OZ (15 G) COFFEE POWDER
2.8 OZ (80 G) SUGAR

FOR THE COFFEE FINE CRUMBLE:
7 OZ (200 G) SOFT FLOUR (00 TYPE FLOUR)
3 OZ (90 G) BUTTER
3 OZ (90 G) SUGAR
0.5 OZ (15 G) COCOA POWDER
0.8 OZ (25 G) COFFEE POWDER

PREPARATION TIME: 30 MINUTES

Melt the chocolate in a bain-marie, maintaining a temperature of 120 °F (50 °C). Remove it from the heat and allow it to cool to 82 °F (28 °c), then bring it back up to 88 °F (31 °C). This process will give the chocolate a glossy shine. Inflate four mini balloons and dip them halfway into the melted chocolate. Place the coated balloons on a small baking tray and refrigerate for 30 minutes. Once the chocolate has cooled, deflate the balloons, leaving you with chocolate demi-spheres that you can use as bowls for the cream and mousse.

For the coffee mousse, mix the cream, coffee, and sugar in a bowl. Pour this mixture into a mousse siphon, shake well, and add one charge. Allow it to set in the refrigerator for 2 hours.

To make the fine coffee crumble, place the flour in a pot and gradually add the room-temperature butter, sugar, cocoa, and coffee while stirring. Keep mixing until you achieve a granular mixture. Bake in the oven at 320 °F (160 °C) for 25 minutes, stirring occasionally. Remove it from the oven, spread the mixture onto a baking sheet, and let it cool at room temperature.

On a plate, spread the fine coffee crumble, then place the chocolate demi-sphere filled with mousse on top. Sprinkle with more fine coffee crumble and serve.

CREAM PANNA COTTA WITH COFFEE SAUCE AND GRANITA

SERVES 4

FOR THE PANNA COTTA:
14 OZ (400 G) WHIPPING CREAM
7 OZ (200 G) FULL FAT MILK
3.5 OZ (100 G) SUGAR
0.3 OZ (9 G) LEAF GELATIN

FOR THE COFFEE GRANITA:
7 OZ (200 G) ESPRESSO COFFEE
2.8 OZ (80 G) SUGAR
0.3 OZ (10 G) HONEY

FOR THE COFFEE SAUCE:
8.8 OZ (250 G) ESPRESSO COFFEE
3.5 OZ (100 G) CASTER SUGAR
0.7 OZ (20 G) BUTTER
0.3 OZ (10 G) CORNSTARCH

PREPARATION TIME: 1 HOUR

For the panna cotta, soak the gelatin leaves in cold water for a few minutes, then drain, squeeze out excess water, and place them in a saucepan with milk, cream, and sugar. Bring the mixture to a boil and strain it through a colander. Divide it into transparent glass molds and refrigerate for 3 hours.

For the granita, pour 7 oz (200 g) of water into a saucepan, add the coffee, sugar, and honey, stir, and cook over low heat until it comes to a boil. Pour the mixture into a shallow oven pan and place it in the freezer for 1 hour.

Stir the mixture, breaking it up with a fork, and return it to the freezer. Repeat this process until it reaches the consistency of granita.

For the coffee cream, combine the butter and cornstarch in a saucepan until you have a smooth mixture. While stirring, add the sugar and coffee. Place it over the heat and bring it to a boil for 1 minute. Then, refrigerate for 2 hours, covering it with plastic wrap.

Whisk the coffee cream thoroughly, then pour a thin layer onto each panna cotta mold to create a coffee disc about 5 mm thick on the surface.

Serve the granita in a separate dish.

PEARS IN VANILLA AND COFFEE SYRUP
WITH YOGURT WAFERS
AND LICORICE POWDER

SERVES 4

FOR THE PEARS:
12 PEARS
1 VANILLA POD
0.2 OZ (8 G) CRUSHED COFFEE BEANS
17 FL OZ (500 ML) WHITE WINE
1 LICORICE ROOT
LEMON ZEST TO TAST

FOR THE YOGURT WAFERS:
9.1 OZ (260 G) SOFT FLOUR (00 TYPE FLOUR)
9.1 OZ (260 G) FULL FAT YOGURT
2 EGGS
1 EGG YOLK
4.2 OZ (120 G) SUGAR
1 PACKET OF ACTIVE DRY YEAST

PREPARATION TIME: 30 MINUTES

Peel the pears and trim the base so that they can stand upright. Place them in a deep pan and add the vanilla, coffee beans, white wine, 17 fl oz (500 ml) of water, and lemon zest. Cook for 50 minutes over low heat, allowing the syrup to simmer. Remove the pears and reduce the remaining syrup by one third. Strain it and then pour it back over the pears.

Grate a licorice root with a fine grater and set the powder aside on a saucer.

Whisk together the eggs, egg yolk, and sugar, then add the yogurt. In a separate bowl, mix the flour and baking powder. Sift them and gradually add them to the wet ingredients. Preheat the oven to 340 °F (170 °C). Transfer the mixture to a pastry bag and pipe it onto a baking sheet lined with parchment paper, forming wafers that are approximately 3x1.5 inches (8x4 cm) in size. Bake for about 10-12 minutes.

Before serving, heat the pears. Place them in a serving bowl and pour the reduced sauce over them. Arrange the freshly baked wafers alongside and sprinkle a little licorice powder on top.

Enjoy your meal!

COFFEE SEMIFREDDO WITH SORREL, CINNAMON SPONGE AND CRUMBLE

SERVES 4

FOR THE SEMIFREDDO:
2 EGG WHITES
2.2 OZ (65 G) CASTER SUGAR
0.7 OZ (20 G) WILDFLOWER HONEY
1.7 OZ (50 G) INSTANT COFFEE
8.8 OZ (250 G) WHIPPING CREAM
A FEW SORREL SPROUTS TO DECORATE

FOR THE CINNAMON SPONGE:
1 EGG
2 EGG YOLKS

1.7 OZ (50 G) SUGAR
0.3 OZ (10 G) WILDFLOWER HONEY
1 OZ (30 G) FLOUR
0.7 OZ (20 G) CORN OIL
0.2 OZ (8 G) FULL FAT MILK
0.1 (3 G) CINNAMON POWDER

FOR THE CRUMBLE:
2.4 OZ (70 G) FLOUR
1.2 OZ (35 G) BROWN SUGAR
1.9 OZ (55 G) COLD BUTTER

PREPARATION TIME: 1 HOUR

For the semifreddo, combine the sugar, 1.4 oz (40 g) of water, and honey in a saucepan and stir. Cook over medium heat until it reaches a temperature of 250 °F (121 °C). In a mixer, pour the egg whites and slowly add the hot syrup while continuing to beat until stiff peaks form. Keep beating until the egg whites reach room temperature. Place the mixture in the fridge to cool. Whip the cream with the coffee and then fold in the egg whites. Transfer the mixture to the appropriate molds and freeze at -0.4 °F (-18 °C) for at least 4 hours.

Wash and dry the sorrel sprouts, then store them in a container with a lid between two sheets of dampened kitchen paper in the fridge.

For the cinnamon sponge, mix the egg, egg yolks, sugar, and honey in a bowl. Stir continuously while adding the oil, milk, and cinnamon. Gradually incorporate the sifted flour to prevent lumps. Pour the mixture into a mousse siphon with two chargers and refrigerate for 4 hours, shaking the siphon occasionally. Grease the ice-cream cups lightly with corn oil. Fill the cups slightly more than halfway with the cinnamon foam and microwave for 1 minute at 800 w. Let the sponge cool and then remove it from the ice-cream cups.

For the crumble, combine sugar, butter, and flour until you have a coarse, lumpy dough. Transfer to a pan and bake at 320 °F (160 °C) for 20 minutes, stirring occasionally to ensure even cooking.

To plate, arrange the semifreddo in the center of the plate, with some foam at the base. Add the sorrel sprouts for their fresh, acidic notes that complement the cinnamon. Sprinkle with crumble for the right crunchiness in the dessert.

Enjoy your delicious dessert!

COFFEE SOUFFLÉ
WITH COFFEE
AND JUNIPER GELATO

SERVES 4

FOR THE COFFEE AND JUNIPER GELATO:
5 EGG YOLKS
3.5 OZ (100 G) CASTER SUGAR
17.6 OZ (500 G) MILK
LEMON ZEST TO TASTE
8 CRUSHED JUNIPER BERRIES
0.5 OZ (15 G) INSTANT COFFEE
1 VANILLA POD
17.6 OZ (500 G) WHIPPING CREAM

FOR THE SOUFFLÉ:
7.7 OZ (220 G) MILK
1.7 OZ (50 G) FLOUR
0.2 OZ (8 G) INSTANT COFFEE
1.5 OZ (45 G) BUTTER
3 EGG YOLKS
3 EGG WHITES
2.1 OZ (60 G) CASTER SUGAR

PREPARATION TIME: 45 MINUTES

For the Gelato Whisk the egg yolks and sugar in a bowl. Heat the milk with lemon zest, coffee, and 4 crushed juniper berries, along with the vanilla, until it's almost boiling. Pour the hot milk into the egg yolk mixture, stirring well to avoid lumps.

Place the bowl in a bain-marie and bring the mixture to a temperature of 180 °F (82 °C), continually stirring with a rubber spatula to prevent sticking. Stir in the whipping cream and let it cool in the fridge for approximately 4 hours, or until it's very cold. Filter the mixture with a strainer.

You can either put the mixture directly into an ice cream maker to solidify, or if you don't have one, leave it in the freezer until it becomes solid. Once it's solid, cut the mixture into cubes and whisk it until it reaches a creamy gelato consistency.

For the Soufflé Melt the butter in a saucepan and, while stirring, gradually add the flour. Let it fry for about 1 minute. Stir in the cold milk all at once, continuing to whisk to avoid lumps. Bring the mixture to a boil and simmer for 3 minutes, stirring thoroughly.

Add the coffee after a few minutes. Incorporate the egg yolks and sugar into the mixture. In a separate bowl, beat the egg whites until stiff peaks form, then gently fold them into the mixture. Grease and flour the soufflé molds, filling them just over halfway. Bake them in a preheated oven at 390 °F (200 °C) for 20 minutes. Pulverize the remaining juniper berries.

Remove the soufflés from the oven and serve them immediately while they're still puffed up.

Place the gelato in a separate dish and sprinkle it with some juniper powder.

ALPHABETICAL INDEX OF RECIPE INGREDIENTS

THE AUTHORS

LUIGI ODELLO, Luigi Odello is an enologist, journalist, and the founder of Odello Associati. He serves as the President of Italian Tasters and the International Institution of Coffee Tasters. Additionally, he holds the position of CEO at Narratori del Gusto and is associated with organizations like Istituto Eccellenze Italiane Certificate, Istituto Internazionale Chocolier, and the Italian Espresso National Institute. He is also the Academic Secretary of the International Academy of Sensory Analysis and sits on the Board of Directors of Absis Consulting and Grappa National Institute. Luigi Odello is the director of publications including *L'Assaggio, Sensory News, Coffee Taster, and Grappa News*. Throughout his career, he has amassed specific expertise in sensory analysis and corporate innovation, with a focus on neuro-linguistic organization and transactional analysis. He dedicates approximately 300 hours per year to university lectures, advises or co-advises over 90 theses, and has authored numerous publications. Luigi Odello has written 19 books, collaborated with leading industry magazines, and presented reports at numerous conventions in Italy and abroad.

FABIO PETRONI Fabio Petroni is a professional photographer who specializes in portraits and still life. He has collaborated with prominent professionals in the photography field and gained experience working with notable figures in Italian culture, medicine, and the economy. He is a sought-after photographer for advertising agencies and has created campaigns for prestigious international firms and companies. Fabio Petroni also plays a key role in shaping the image of renowned Italian brands. He serves as the official photographer for the IJRC (International Jumping Riders Club) and the Young Riders Academy. Furthermore, he has authored several prestigious publications in collaboration with White Star Publishers. *www.fabiopetronistudio.com*

GIOVANNI RUGGIERI, Giovanni Ruggieri was born in Bethlehem in 1984 but was raised in Piedmont. He received professional training in various Michelin-starred kitchens, including those at Piazza Duomo in Alba and Scrigno del Duomo in Trento. Currently, he serves as the chef at Refettorio Simplicitas, an elegantly refined restaurant located in Milan's Brera district. Ruggieri is dedicated to promoting a culinary approach based on simplicity, with a strong emphasis on the quality of raw materials. He selects ingredients based on seasonality and authenticity, incorporating niche products from his region. Ruggieri's cooking style is characterized by simplicity, sobriety, balance, and a touch of asceticism.

HOW TO LEARN COFFEE TASTING

The International Institute of Coffee Tasters (Iiac) is a non-profit association funded solely through its members' subscriptions. Its primary objective is to research and promote scientific methods for the sensory evaluation of coffee, with a particular focus on espresso, which symbolizes the "Made in Italy" tradition. Since its establishment in 1993, Iiac has organized numerous Italian Espresso Tasting courses that have attracted participants from around the world, including coffee industry professionals and enthusiasts. In 1999, Iiac introduced the Italian Espresso Specialist course, designed to certify individuals working in coffee shops serving Certified Italian Espresso. In 2005, they inaugurated the Professional Master's Degree in Coffee Science and Sensory Analysis, furthering their commitment to coffee education. In 2012, the Italian Espresso Trainer program was established to train ambassadors of Italian coffee. Iiac's research initiatives benefit from the expertise of a distinguished scientific committee. The Italian Espresso Tasting manual is available in multiple languages, including Italian, English, German, French, Spanish, Portuguese, Russian, Japanese, Chinese, Thai, and Korean.

For more information on courses and activities offered by Iiac, please visit their website at: *www.assaggiatoricaffe.org.*

BIBLIOGRAPHY

Luigi Odello, Carlo Odello, *Espresso Italiano Tasting* (edition I), Centro Studi Assaggiatori, 2001

Luigi Odello, Carlo Odello, *Espresso Italiano Tasting* (edition II), Centro Studi Assaggiatori, 2017

Luigi Odello, *Espresso Italiano Roasting,* Centro Studi Assaggiatori, 2009

Luigi Odello, *I cru del caffè,* Centro Studi Assaggiatori, 2013

Luigi Odello, Manuela Violoni, *Sensory analysis. The psychophysiology of perception*, Centro Studi Assaggiatori, 2017

Silvano Bontempo, *Dal chicco alla tazzina un piacere senza confini,* L'Assaggio

Manuela Violoni, *Il cappuccino italiano certificato,* L'Assaggio

Francesco and Riccardo Illy, *The Book of Coffee: A Gourmet's Guide*, Abbeville Pr, 1992

Antonio Carbè, *Il caffè nella storia e nell'arte* (seconda edizione), Centro Luigi Lavazza

Maria Linardi, Enrico Maltoni, Manuel Terzi, *Il libro completo del caffè*, DeAgostini, 2005

PHOTO CREDITS

All photographs are by Fabio Petroni except the following:

page 8 Jeremy Woodhouse/Blend Images/Getty Images
page 13 Nattika/Shutterstock
page 16 Robert George Young/Getty Images
pags 18-19 Maximilian Stock Ltd./Getty Images
page 20 Ann Ronan Pictures/Print Collector/Getty Images
pages 22-23 Nenov/Getty Images
page 24 Fine Art Images/Heritage Images/Getty Images
page 25 Neil Fletcher & Matthew Ward/Dorling Kindersley/Getty Images
page 27 Jesse Kraft/123RF
page 28 Reza/AGF/Hemis
pages 40-41 John Coletti/Getty Images
pages 42-43 Dick Davis/Science Source/Getty Images
pages 44-45 Ed Gifford/Royalty-free/Getty Images
page 46 Alvis Upitis/Passage/Getty Images
page 48-49 Ze Martinusso/Moment Open/Getty Images
page 50-51 Oleksandr Rupeta/NurPhoto/Getty Images

page 52-53 Paula Bronstein/Getty Images
pages 54-55 Bartosz Hadyniak/E+/Getty Images
page 57 Bill Gentile/Corbis Documentary/Getty Images
pages 58-59 Reza/Getty Images
pages 60-61 Reza/Getty Images
pages 64-65 Reza/Getty Images
page 74 alextype/123RF
page 76 Robert Przybysz/123RF
pages 78-79 Vladimir Shulevsky/StockFood Creative/Getty Images
page 156 Evannovostro/Shutterstock
page 163 republica/E+/Getty Images
page 165 Popperfoto/Getty Images
page 189 ansonsaw/E+/Getty Images
page 191 StockFood/Getty Images

Cover and backcover bottom: Joseph Clark/Getty Images

ACKNOWLEDGEMENTS

The Editor wishes to thank for their valuable collaboration in the making of this book:
MILANI S.p.A. and Elisabetta Milani for their dedication in carrying out the photo shoot.
Mumac Academy and Gruppo Cimbali S.P.A., and Luigi Morello and Filippo Mazzoni for their support in realizing the pictures.
The Taster Study Centre.
Simone Bergamaschi, assistant to Fabio Petroni.
Davide Canonica, kitchen assistant.
Villa Giù of Faggeto Lario, Como for Chef Giovanni Ruggieri's recipes.

For permission requests, please contact the publisher at:

Mango Publishing Group
2850 Douglas Road, 2nd Floor
Coral Gables, FL 33134 USA
info@mango.bz

For special orders, quantity sales, course adoptions and corporate sales, please email the publisher at sales@mango.bz. For trade and wholesale sales, please contact Ingram Publisher Services at customer. service@ingramcontent.com or +1.800.509.4887.

Why We Love Coffee: Fun Facts, History, and Culture of World's Most Popular Drink

ISBN (pb) 978-1-68481-384-1 (hc) 978-1-68481-385-8 (e) 978-1-68481-386-5
LCCN: has been requested
BISAC: CKB019000, COOKING / Beverages / Coffee & Tea

Printed in the United States of America